Austerity Ireland

Austerity Ireland

The Failure of Irish Capitalism

Kieran Allen with Brian O' Boyle

PlutoPress
www.plutobooks.com

First published 2013 by Pluto Press
345 Archway Road, London N6 5AA

www.plutobooks.com

Distributed in the United States of America exclusively by
Palgrave Macmillan, a division of St. Martin's Press LLC,
175 Fifth Avenue, New York, NY 10010

British Library Cataloguing in Publication Data
A catalogue record for this book is available from the British Library

ISBN 978 0 7453 3401 1 Paperback
ISBN 978 0 7453 3402 8 Hardback
ISBN 978 1 8496 4954 4 PDF eBook
ISBN 978 1 8496 4956 8 Kindle eBook
ISBN 978 1 8496 4955 1 EPUB eBook

Library of Congress Cataloging in Publication Data applied for
This book is printed on paper suitable for recycling and made from
fully managed and sustained forest sources. Logging, pulping and
manufacturing processes are expected to conform to the
environmental standards of the country of origin.

10 9 8 7 6 5 4 3 2 1

Typeset from disk by Swales & Willis
Simultaneously printed digitally by CPI Antony Rowe,
Chippenham, UK and
Edwards Bros in the United States of America

Contents

Tables

1

Wreckage

What happens when a government goes to a failed Wall Street mogul for advice in a crisis?

In September 2008, money was pouring out of Irish banks as news spread about a property bubble that was collapsing. The government panicked, thinking that the ATM machines might seize up and there would be riots on the streets. So they put through a call to Merrill Lynch for advice. The Wall Street giant seemed to be as solid a corporation as you could possibly get. Originally formed as a network of stockbrokers selling to middle class Americans, it had a host of Irish Catholics at its helm. With this connection to the 'old country', it seemed the right place to look for advice. In fact, it should have been the very last. Merrill Lynch was a dealer in toxic sub-prime securities – and it was sinking fast. Stung by the success of its rival, Goldman Sachs, it had been packaging up the mortgages of poor people as Triple-A-Rated Collateralised Debt Obligations. It made a fortune in fees from selling these on to finance houses around the world who thought they could collect a steady income flow. But Merrill Lynch's luck ran out in 2008 and it was stuck holding €45 billion worth of its own dodgy financial products. By the time the Irish government came knocking on its door for advice, it was losing €52 million dollars a day.[1] Two weeks before it wrote up its advice to the Irish government, it was taken over by Bank of America.

If this sounds like a *Father Ted*-style comedy, it was to get even more farcical. Merrill Lynch had a lucrative relationship with Irish banks and had been covering up for them. It was the underwriter for Anglo-Irish bonds and a corporate broker for Allied Irish Bank, earning huge fees for its efforts. In March 2008, one of its younger banking analysts, Phil Ingram, examined the commercial loans of Irish banks and concluded that a major write-down was in the offing. Within hours, the report flew all around the London financial markets and the executives of the Irish banks were fuming. They rang Merrill Lynch and the Ingram report was censored, softened and re-edited before being released with a different story-line.[2]

Merrill Lynch charged the Irish government €7 million for its 14-page advisory document – a neat half a million a page. It made one claim that was to shape the destiny of Ireland for years and, maybe, decades afterwards. 'It is important to stress', Merrill Lynch noted, 'that at present, liquidity concerns aside, all of the Irish banks are profitable and well capitalised'.[3] In other words they were fundamentally sound and were only suffering a cash flow problem. They reported that 97 per cent of Anglo-Irish loans were 'neither impaired nor past due'[4] – although they qualified this with reference to possible property price falls. Written in typical business-speak, the Merrill Lynch memorandum provided a number of options, including a state guarantee for the six domestic banks.[5] But once the problem was framed as a temporary cash flow problem, state aid became a logical 'solution'. Some caveats were expressed, but it did not seem to matter greatly that the sums involved were huge.

The Irish banks had been gambling on an enormous scale because friendly politicians had changed laws to facilitate them. Instead of just taking in deposits from Irish savers, they had been issuing bonds – or IOUs – to the global money markets to increase their loan book. In 2001, the Dail had passed an Assets Covered Securities Act to allow banks to issue 'covered' bonds. This meant that creditors were guaranteed that they would be first to have access to the underlying mortgage payments. The law was described as a 'benchmark' for European legislation[6] and it gave the banks a huge flow of credit from British and German financial institutions. Incredibly, the legislation had been drafted with the help of the Irish Banking Federation and a partner in McCann Fitzgerald, a big legal firm.[7]

Banks and drug dealers have one thing in common – the more they addict their clients, the more they gain. The addiction can be to loans or drugs – but the main thing is to dole it out and get the clients hooked. Just as the small time drug pusher expands by getting more gear from a bigger supplier, so too did the banks want more loanable cash. In 2007, at the height of the Celtic Tiger boom, Irish banks had lent out €342 billion. Incredibly, this was more than twice the size of the Irish economy and was far higher than the €166 billion they held in deposits.[8] The shortfall was made up by a vast amount of money that came through bonds. When, in September 2008, the Irish state issued a blanket guarantee on these bonds, it made its own people liable for the vast private debts. It had gone to a failed Wall Street gambler for advice on how to help their friends in Dublin and, naturally, the option of a state hand-out was suggested. If the regulars who frequent the Paddy Power bookie shops had gone to state officials for help with their 'cash flow problems', they would have been laughed out of court. But when private banks, who gambled on an enormous scale, did the same thing, they were treated with deference and respect.

Another firm which was heavily involved in the state guarantee decision was Arthur Cox. This is one of the most lucrative legal firms in Europe, because it gets big contracts from the Irish state and the financial industry. It used to be the main legal agent for Anglo Irish Bank and was currently acting as the main lawyer for Bank of Ireland.[9] But none of this was regarded as a conflict of interest. After all, the firm had also won the contract to be the lead legal provider for the Health Services Executive at the very time that its chairperson, Eugene McCague, served on its board. According to the firm, it was just a matter of preserving a Chinese Wall between the different wings of the same firm. Arthur Cox went on to become a major beneficiary of the Irish financial crisis. Between 2008 and 2011, it received €13.5 million from the Department of Finance for banking advice, including helping to draw up a law guaranteeing bank debts.[10] It got another €7.4 million for helping to set up the National Asset Management Agency (NAMA), the state agency charged with hoovering up the bad debts of the Irish banks.[11] Then it got €3.07 million in legal fees from NAMA between 2010 and 2011.[12] And when the future pension funds of Irish workers were stuffed into Allied Irish Bank and Bank of Ireland, Arthur Cox was again at hand, collecting another €2.1 million to ease the flow. Who says that dark clouds do not have silver linings?

One other firm involved in the crisis decision making meetings was Goldman Sachs. It met with the government on 21 September 2008 to discuss the situation at Irish Nationwide Building Society. It noted that there was 'lots of reassurance' that the building society's loan book had 'real value' but claimed it was facing a 'liquidity problem' and suggested that 'help from the authorities will be required'.[13] This was an extremely grave miscalculation, because the bailout of Irish Nationwide eventually cost the Irish state over €5.4 billion. Yet Goldman Sachs, the doyen of the financial engineering industry rode off into the sunset, leaving the Irish people to pick up the tab.

The decision to guarantee private bank debts was the greatest calamity that ever befell the Irish people. It occurred because the state surrounded itself with advisors drawn from corporations and took their advice uncritically. Global capitalism was going down the tubes because of financial speculation – and whom did they turn to? The speculators. The fat cats of the world were panicking over losses and what did the Irish government worry about? Restoring the 'confidence of the financial markets'. Politicians often talk blandly about 'thinking outside the box' and being 'innovative' but when you get right down to it in a crisis, they thought there was only one natural thing to do – talk to the people with the money.

Corporate Ireland

This attitude of deference to the corporate elite runs deep in official Ireland. The country marketed itself as a free enterprise paradise that offered light touch regulation and a host of tax breaks. It 'ticked the boxes' on adhering to formal rules but turned a blind eye to all sorts of ruthless business practices. That way, corporations could gain an aura of respectability while having the freedom to do as they pleased. The country was the very model of a neoliberal economy, hailed by market fundamentalists as a success story *because* it cut taxes and did not interfere with business. In 2007, at the height of the boom, Ireland was ranked number three in an Index of Economic Freedom, drawn up by two mouthpieces of the neoliberals, the Heritage Foundation and the *Wall Street Journal*. It scored nine out of ten for 'business freedom', 'financial freedom' and 'investment freedom'. That was nearly top of the class for gung ho, unrestrained capitalism. Writing in the *New York Times*, the economist Paul Krugman summed it up.

How did Ireland get into its current bind? By being just like us, (Americans) only more so. Like its near namesake, Iceland, Ireland jumped with both feet into the brave world of unsupervised global markets. Last year the Heritage Foundation declared Ireland the third freest economy in the world, behind only Hong Kong and Singapore.[14]

During the Celtic Tiger era, the media drooled over the achievements of Irish entrepreneurs. Businesspeople were given their own slot every morning on RTE news – Business News – to crow about their achievements. Game shows like *The Apprentice* or *Dragons' Den* were designed as fantasy programmes to romanticise business 'leaders' and suck people into an aspiration to emulate them. Bill Cullen – a former Renault car dealer – was given endless opportunities to tell his rags to riches story so that he could be held up as a model for, what he termed, the 'mollycoddled youth'.[15] Aside from the US, Singapore and Hong Kong, there was hardly another country that extolled commercial values more than Celtic Tiger Ireland.

This culture was the seedbed from which the decision to bail out banks had sprung and it was no accident because the political elite were intimately linked to the big corporations. They saw nothing unusual about surrounding themselves with big money people or 'financial engineers'. If anyone inside their charmed circles had the temerity to suggest that the banks should be nationalised and their debts repudiated, they would have been called a 'head-banger' and shown the door. That question never even arose, however, because the crisis was framed as a matter of 'restoring confidence' to the financial system. Banks were supposed to be the 'lifeblood' of an economy and had to be helped. End of story. After the event, a different story-line grew that it was all down to Brian Cowen and his incompetent advisors in the Department of Finance. Fianna Fail apparently caused the crisis because they were so used to looking after their insider friends among bankers and developers they did not see the bigger picture. No doubt, there were important ties between Fianna Fail and Anglo Irish Bank in particular, but blaming particular individuals is a way of absolving the entire system. You just throw out a few fall guys so things stay as they are. The reality, however, was that the two main parties Fianna Fail and

Fine Gael voted for the bank guarantee scheme – alongside Sinn Fein. Richard Bruton of Fine Gael summed up the overwhelming consensus.

It is important that we copper fasten our financial system. We must all understand that a sound financial system is like the oil running through an engine. If that oil is drained away by a loss of confidence, then suddenly that engine seizes and the problems that beset people . . . get much worse.[16]

The Labour Party voted against the measure but they accepted that 'drastic action' was needed to keep credit flowing. Their main criticism was that the Minister had taken too many powers and not answered enough questions. Somewhat bizarrely, Ruairi Quinn suggested that there was 'blatant discrimination' against non-Irish banks because they would not be covered by the guarantee.[17]

The decision to guarantee the €440 billion debts of Irish banks was a hare-brained scheme. It was supposed to be a cute move to get ahead of other states and ensure that credit kept flowing into Irish banks. At the time, the financial world was stuck in a 'credit crunch' as banks would not lend to each other. The Irish government thought it could solve this difficulty with a guarantee of repayment and so hoover in credit to keep the Irish banks afloat. The scheme worked for a few weeks but then the worm turned. Why, some of the financiers asked, was this guarantee necessary if the banks were sound? And could a small economy really guarantee debts that were three times the size of its economy? Billions began to flow out again and the state was hoisted on its own petard. Its fate became intertwined with the banks and so a chain of calamitous events began to unfold.

The first sign of what was ahead came when a new word entered the vocabulary as the elite started to talk about 'recapitalisation'. This was a strange business term for pouring the people's money into banks. In other circumstances this money – which was raised from taxes and borrowing – might be used to build schools or hospitals but 'recapitalisation' meant the banks had first call on it. In December 2008, there was a recapitalisation of three banks to the tune of €5.5 billion; another €7 billion was needed three months later; then another €4 billion for Anglo Irish Bank in May 2009; then in March 2010 another €2.7 billion for Irish Nationwide and €8 billion for Anglo; and back to Irish Nationwide again for another €2.7 billion and so on. On 1 April 2011– appropriately April Fool's Day – the media reported an important pronouncement from the Central Bank. Yet another €24 billion in total would be needed to bail out banks, bringing it all to a grand total of over €64 billion. The endless talk of billions led to dazed eyes everywhere. Once upon a time people were told the country could not afford a *million* to save a few hospital beds or to replace a prefab classroom. Yet suddenly billions upon billions became available because very important people in banks were talking about their 'life blood' and 'confidence'. The cost of the bailouts was the equivalent to the people of Ireland working for nearly six months for free – as slaves, for no wages. Of course, the slave duty could be spread out over their lifetime and onto their children's – but pay for it they must with their time and labour.

Then there was nationalisation. This had been ruled out in 2009, with the government's special economics advisor, Alan Ahearne, arguing that it would scare off the international markets. 'It would be taken as a sign that the banking systems have completely failed', he boldly declared.[18] Yet within two years, five of the six Irish banks had fallen under state control. The only one remaining in private hands was Bank of Ireland and this only occurred because the state handed over its 35 per cent share to a Canadian company, Fairfax Financial, for a mere €1.1 billion – even though it had put €4.2 billion of public funds into the bank since the crisis. Nationalisation is often thought of as a left-wing policy but that is only when it is a device to take assets of the wealthy into public ownership. The nationalisation of Irish banks was about taking control of debt – not assets. The Irish state took on debts of private gamblers and made them its own. During the Celtic Tiger, Bank of Ireland, Allied Irish Bank and Anglo Irish Bank made over a billion euros every year in profit, but the Irish state received very little because tax rates were so low. There was no talk of sharing the profits with society because there could be no interference in the market. Yet, when the crash happened the rhetoric changed and 'we' all had to share the burden of paying off bad debts.

The insane policy of bailing out banks has had four major, overlapping effects.

First, it pushed up government debt. In 2007, just before the crash, Irish sovereign debt stood at €47 billion, which amounted to a quarter of its GDP. There was nothing unusual about this and in fact, it was a good deal better than many other countries. Germany, for example, which is held up as a model of financial discipline had a much higher debt ratio, the equivalent of two-thirds of its GDP. After the bailout, however, the Irish national debt shot up to €192 billion, which was the equivalent of 118 per cent of GDP.[19] This debt will hold Irish society in a vice grip for years to come. Second, this level of debt entails high interest payments every year. In 2012, interest on the national debt amounted to €6.3 billion and it was set to rise to over €9 billion a year by 2015. However, a deal on the 'promissory note' that the Irish government used to fund the Anglo Irish bailout subsequently reduced the interest payments – but only at the cost of lengthening the payment period to 2053. From 2022, interest payments will rise to €10 billion for the next decade and €14 billion in the decade after that.

Third, funds that were put in reserve to pay for future pensions have been blown away on banks. Almost €20.7 billion was taken out of the National Pension Reserve Fund (NPRF) and used to buy shares in Allied Irish Bank and Bank of Ireland. These shares were virtually worthless so as soon as they were purchased, the original values declined considerably. The NPRF claims that its portfolio holding in these two banks amounts to only €8.1 billion.[20] In other words, it has already lost more than €12 billion of money that should have been used to pay for pensions. Further state money was used to purchase shares in other banks and when account is taken of all these, the economist Karl Whelan estimates that the loss to the national pension fund will come to a total of €17 billion.[21] Future pensioners will experience poverty and suffering because of this criminal waste of the savings of Irish society. Yet there was a small consolation for some. The government nominated three politicians from a bygone era, Dick Spring, Ray MacSharry and Joe Walsh, to sit on bank boards as directors. Between them they raked in €453,000 in fees to add to their handsome Ministerial pensions. They at least would be looked after in their old age.

Finally, NAMA tied the fortunes of the Irish state to the property market – and to the developers who hyped it up. The Irish state spent

€32 billion to allow NAMA to take toxic loans off the banks. These loans were supposed to be backed by assets which had a notional value of €74 billion and the agency was charged with getting full recovery of the debt. It quickly transpired, however, that NAMA was only seeking to recover its original €32 billion and it thought that the best way to ensure this was to co-operate with some of the developers. Simon Carswell of the *Irish Times* has named the top ten borrowers who transferred loans to NAMA after the crash. What was astounding was that they each had an average borrowing of €1.6 billion:

> They are developers Liam Carroll; Bernard McNamara; Sean Mulryan of Ballymore; financier Derek Quinlan; Paddy McKillen, owner of the Jervis Street Shopping Centre; Treasury Holdings, which is owned by Johnny Ronan and Richard Barrett; Cork developer Michael O'Flynn; Joe O'Reilly, the developer behind the Dundrum Shopping Centre in Dublin; Dublin builder Gerry Gannon, co-owner of the K Club golf resort in Co Kildare; and Galway businessman Gerry Barrett, owner of Ashford Castle in Co Mayo and the G Hotel in Galway.[22]

A strange alliance between NAMA and some of the developers began to unfold in a variety of ways. In the first instance, €3.5 billion was made available to the developers in generous loan facilities to complete some of their projects.[23] This was a particularly useful privilege as not many financial institutions would provide credit to individuals with such high levels of debt. Sixty-six developers were also paid salaries of over €100,000 a year to work with the agency.[24] In a more substantial sweetener, 41 debtors received an average of more than €1 million each in 'overhead costs' for repairing or improving their own properties.[25] There was also a light touch approach to the collection on the rents from these properties. Nine million euro a month is paid on rent for NAMA properties in Ireland, but these funds are not automatically impounded to pay off the loans.[26] Instead developers appeared able to keep a substantial portion for the repair and maintenance of the properties. Moreover, some of the developers came to believe they only have to pay NAMA the discounted rate at which the agency purchased their debts.[27] So if they borrowed, say, €500 million from Bank of

Ireland and NAMA purchased this debt at a discount rate of €250 million, then it is the lower figure that has to be paid back.

The bank bailout has been truly disastrous on many levels but as the country sank ever deeper into economic and social depression, there was one last sting in the tail. The events of September 2008 eventually led to the Troika arriving in late November 2010. Officially this was deemed a necessary support for the Irish economy. In reality our so-called partners were here to rescue their friends in the European banking system.

2

The Partners

Initially, the decision to guarantee the debt of six Irish banks seemed to catch everyone on the hop. The Irish elites had pulled a fast one on their taxpayers and not even the European Central Bank (ECB) appeared to be in on the act. When told about the plan, French Finance Minister, Christine Lagarde, supposedly exclaimed 'Oh my God'[1] and her British counterpart was reported to be similarly alarmed.[2] However, the bankers at the heart of the ECB were in far more command of the situation than it first appeared. Whatever the Irish government may have announced, the state guarantee would have no effect until it could be given proper legal standing. This meant enacting legislation and the ECB made it clear that it 'expected to be consulted on any proposals . . . that materially influenced the stability of financial markets and institutions'.[3] It further insisted that 'the (EU) commissions' opinion be appropriately. . . reflected in the Irish legislative and regulatory framework adopted under law'.[4] This effectively pushed European bankers and bureaucrats into the heart of the crisis decision making from the very start. Absolutely nothing could have happened without EU sanction as an EU Commission statement made abundantly clear:

> The commission acknowledges that in the current context there is an international market-failure . . . Banks have lost confidence in lending to each other given the risk of failure is too high. This risk is avoided by the current guarantee scheme . . . In addition, by fully guaranteeing deposits the measure at issue is able to restore depositors' trust in the banking system and avoid bank runs. Thus, the *commission considers that the guarantee is an appropriate remedy to a serious disturbance to the Irish economy.*[5]

The context referred to was the credit crunch in financial markets precipitated by the collapse of Lehman Brothers.[6] This crisis had been triggered by a collapse in US sub-prime mortgages but it quickly spread throughout global capitalism. European powerhouses such as Deutsche Bank, BNP Paribas and Societe Generale had enthusiastically diversified into the complex financial instruments that facilitated most of the sub-prime lending and these were responsible for much of the bankers' astronomical profits. However, by the middle of 2008 their speculative adventures were coming badly unstuck. Deutsche Industriebank (IKB) was the first European bank to fall seriously foul of market sentiment.[7] This process soon gained momentum and by the end of 2008 Germany's three worst affected banks had lost $41.1 billion, their British counterparts were down $31.8 billion, whilst Naxis, BNP Paribas and UBS suffered losses of over $70 billion.[8] The core of the European banking system was rapidly disintegrating and it is in this context that the EU sanctioned Ireland's blanket bank guarantee scheme.

During the Celtic Tiger, Irish banks had facilitated their own orgy of speculative lending. Patrick Honohan, the current governor of the Irish Central Bank, has estimated that the six guaranteed banks increased their 'assets' from around €85 billion in 1999 to just under €600 billion in 2008.[9] This figure, more than 17 times the current Irish tax-take (€34 billion) shows just how reckless the guarantee scheme really was. If any of the bigger banks were to prove insolvent, the sheer weight of the losses could bankrupt the country. This should have been uppermost in the minds of European regulators, but in the event it was the *sources* of the Irish funds that proved crucial in their deliberations. According to the Bank for International Settlements, Ireland's lenders had sourced the vast bulk of their funds from their European counterparts. Between them French and German corporations pumped €185 billion into the Irish financial system, with a further €113 billion spilling in from the UK.[10] In total, Irish banks borrowed €433 billion from their European creditors, making some form of guarantee scheme absolutely essential. From the outset, the health of European banks has been the key consideration in EU decision making. The ECB, in particular was hell-bent on stabilising the financial system with a series of manoeuvres that have effectively pushed the costs of the crisis onto working people. This dovetailed perfectly with the needs of Irish capitalism, which has traditionally been heavily concentrated in banking and construction.

The bank guarantee scheme set off a series of events that eventually culminated in an €85 billion 'bailout' of the Irish economy from the International Monetary Fund (IMF), the EU and the ECB. To many it seemed that this 'Troika' of international creditors could hardly do a worse job than the corrupt Irish political establishment. In reality, they have worked hand in glove to force through a programme of austerity that comes right out of the IMF's playbook. Since the late 1970s, the IMF has acted as the chief enforcer for financial capital and has helped to pump trillions out of the poorest people in the world. Now the Troika was coming to restructure Ireland and the record of its individual components showed just what was in store.

Who Are the Troika?

IMF

The International Monetary Fund (IMF) was one of a series of financial institutions established at the Bretton Woods Conference in 1944 alongside the World Bank. There was considerable pressure to found these institutions on the basis of one country, one vote. However, such was the power of the US that voting rights immediately became linked to contributions in a quota system.[11] In other words, the more that a country put into the fund as loan capital – the higher the number of votes it received. Currently, the US has 17 per cent of the votes at the IMF and this gives it a veto on any policy that might adversely affect its interests.

The IMF operated by disciplining countries that fell into arrears but it left those countries running persistent trade surpluses immune from sanction. Generous loans were also lavished on governments that were friendly to Western interests, as the 'Fund' and the 'Bank' steadily built up a network of clients. Central to this strategy was an appeal to the privileged positions of the elites in poorer countries. Western bankers were happy to profit from genuine development strategies, but they were equally happy to fund the military adventures of right-wing dictatorships. The key was to gain traction over Third World nations whilst gradually (re)incorporating them into the Western orbit. Throughout the 1950s and 1960s the IMF worked hard to ensure that global development was sanctioned and controlled by Western bankers. This often proved challenging in the context of Third World nationalism, but by the early 1970s the IMF came into its own.

In 1973, the Organization of the Petroleum Exporting Countries (OPEC) (an oil cartel dominated by Arab nations) restricted its oil supply in retaliation for US support of Israel during the Yom Kippur War. Within months the price of oil quadrupled, from $3 a barrel to $12 a barrel, and much of the world slid into recession. Massive trade surpluses in the oil-producing countries were deposited in Western banks. Anxious to make a killing, Wall Street bankers quickly recycled the so-called 'petro-dollars' as loans into the coffers of Third World treasuries. However, as growth faltered and interest rates skyrocketed, increasing numbers of debtors began to struggle with their loans.[12] By 1978, the IMF had already approved more than one hundred emergency loans for developing countries.[13] From $75 billion in 1972, Latin American debt exploded to more than $315 billion by 1982. This represented more than 50 per cent of the region's GDP and was clearly unsustainable. Moreover, debt servicing (interest payments and the repayment of principal) had grown even faster, increasing from $12 to $66 billion in the seven years to 1982.[14] Something simply had to give. In August 1982, Mexico announced that it could no longer make its loan repayments. Brazil soon made a similar announcement and fearing the consequences for US banks, the Reagan administration decided to act.[15] In conjunction with the US Treasury, Reagan tasked the IMF with restructuring Latin American debt in return for what has since become known as structural adjustment.[16] The IMF has always attached some level of 'conditionality' to its loans, but now recipient economies were to be *entirely restructured* in a process that forced much of the developing world back into colonial servitude.

The first principle in any structural adjustment programme is the population always pays.[17] Despite their reckless lending, the Western bankers got their money back in full, making significant profits in the process.[18] In return for its loans, the IMF got crucial leverage over government policy and it used this to prize open the peripheral economies. By the mid 1980s, three decades of relatively autonomous industrialisation were being dismantled as three-quarters of Latin America and two-thirds of Africa were under strict supervision.[19] In a philosophy that became known as the Washington Consensus, the IMF and World Bank consistently prescribed a combination of (1) fiscal and monetary discipline, (2) currency devaluations, (3) labour market flexibilisation, (4) privatisation, and (5) liberalisation in trade and capital flows.[20] Taken together, these policies would supposedly free up entrepreneurial energy in developing countries, whilst encouraging the capital and expertise of Western corporations.

Fiscal discipline meant reorienting the state away from what was deemed to be 'wasteful' public spending. This led to large reductions in welfare provisions, dismantling of food and energy subsidies and drastic cuts in health and education spending.[21] A key mechanism was the introduction of 'user fees' for basic public services. Poor people were particularly affected and a subsequent World Bank report on Zambia had to acknowledge that 'vulnerable groups seem to have been denied access to health services.'[22] Simultaneously, the recipient government was tasked with facilitating foreign investment and promoting exports by devaluing the currency. Laws that gave some protection to workers were removed in order to reduce wages, whilst privatisation was encouraged to bring in revenue for the state. Each of these policies would undoubtedly increase inequality but the Fund was confident that a 'rising tide would soon lift all boats' as it 'helped countries to adopt economic policies that can raise the growth rate of per capita incomes on a sustainable basis'.[23] The IMF also claimed to be 'fully committed to . . . making a dent in global poverty'.[24] But the evidence on both counts reveals a very different story.

According to an extensive survey by the United Nations Conference on Trade and Development (UNCTAD) of the 48 least developed countries in which structural adjustment was the main determinant of economic policy, 'average real GDP was stagnant in the three years after the programme was initiated and then actually began to fall by 1.1 per cent per annum in the following three years'. [25] Joseph Stiglitz, Nobel Laureate and former chief economist of the World Bank, is even more emphatic, arguing that 'Half a century after its founding , it is clear that the IMF has failed in its mission . . . capital market liberal-isation has been pushed despite the fact that there is no evidence showing it spurs economic growth'.[26] Even Johnson and Schaefer, of the arch-conservative Heritage Foundation, have been forced to admit that

> forty-eight of eighty-nine countries that received IMF money between 1965 and 1995 are no better off economically than they were before; of these, thirty-two are poorer than before; and fourteen of these are at least 15 per cent smaller than they were before the first IMF loan.[27]

The promised growth is nowhere to be seen. Meanwhile, the combined effects of restricting state supports, slashing wages, devaluing the currency and reducing social services was to throw whole populations into misery. Figures developed by Budhoo estimate the deaths of children in Latin America, Asia and Africa directly attributable to IMF austerity at 6 million every year.[28] Jubilee 2000, a faith-based organ-isation has argued that it is closer to 7 million.[29] In all of this, sub-Saharan Africa has been particularly badly affected with per capita incomes often falling by 25 per cent or more.[30] *Africa Action* takes up the human tragedy that has resulted:

> The removal of food and agricultural subsidies . . . created increased food insecurity. This led to a marked deterioration in nutritional status especially among women and children (thus) providing fertile ground for HIV/AIDS and other infectious diseases . . . Cutbacks in health budgets and privatisation of health services eroded advances in healthcare made after independence and resulted in the closure of hundreds of clinics, hospitals and medical facilities . . . Consequently, during the past two decades the life expectancy of Africans has dropped by fifteen years.[31]

This amounts to little more than IMF-sanctioned genocide and such has been their destructive force that prominent activist Raj Patel has denounced structural adjustment policies as 'weapons of mass destruc-tion, far more powerful than any bomb and insidious in the silent way that they go about killing'.[32] Meanwhile, corporate and financial interests have benefited tremendously from IMF and World Bank interventions. David Harvey has estimated that since 1980 the equivalent of over $4.6 trillion have been sent by the peoples at the periphery to their creditors in the centre.[33] Harvey claims that this was the intention from the very outset, as the US Treasury–Wall Street– IMF complex set about pillaging resources from the global South.[34] Specifically this meant appealing to the privileged self-interest of the rulers of poorer countries whilst using debt to gain leverage over their natural resources. In return they have turned a blind eye to human rights abuses, protected the assets of dictators and provided copious amounts of military hardware.[35]

EU

The European Union (EU) was once seen as a benign institution that brought peace to the continent of Europe and ensured that all countries gained from economic progress. In reality, it has always been domi- nated by the big states with the most powerful corporations on the European mainland.[36] Over time a growing periphery was gradually added, but from the outset it was the most advanced sections of European capital that would drive the process of integration.[37] This inevitably left a serious democratic deficit at the heart of the decision making process. Within the EU the elected parliament has never had any right to propose legislation. This has been reserved for a full-time bureaucracy run by an unelected group of Commissioners. Neither of these bodies is directly accountable to European citizens. In contrast, there are literally thousands of full-time lobbyists working on behalf of the big corporations. The key ones are the Association for the Monetary Union of Europe, which is the bankers' lobby, and the European Roundtable of Industrialists, which represents the top businesspeople.

The EU Commission was determined to use the crash of 2008 to undermine democracy further. They set up a regime of economic surveillance whereby every country would be subject to a tight list of measurements devised by the EU bureaucracy. As José Manuel Barroso explained, 'What is going on is a silent revolution in terms of stronger economic governance by small steps'.[38] In some cases, the EU promoted this strategy of surveillance by means of 'soft coups'. They pushed aside elected Prime Ministers – of both the social democratic Left and the populist Right – who did not comply with their demands and replaced them with technocrats. In Italy, for example, EU Council President, Herman Van Rompuy said 'the country needed reforms, not elections'.[39] The Italian Prime Minister Berlusconi was told to leave and replaced by a professional economist, Mario Monti, who had been a former advisor to Goldman Sachs, Coca-Cola and the rating agency Moody's. However, the main mechanism used by the EU bureaucracy to gain control was a 'lock-in' strategy. They set up time frames where governments were supposed to introduce 'structural reforms' and also created 'score-cards' to show measurable progress on reducing items such as 'unit labour costs'. A major example of these structural reforms was raising the retirement age of European workers to 68.

For the EU Commission, the Memorandums of Understanding imposed on Ireland after the Troika's loan would only be the start of a new, long-term mode of capitalist rule.

ECB

The European Central Bank (ECB) is the primary guardian of monetary policy within the Eurozone. Based in Frankfurt, the ECB is expected to monitor prices, regulate interest rates and support the integrity of the single currency. The ECB presents itself as a technical institution working on behalf of citizens across the Eurozone. In reality, it is a highly political instrument in the hands of big business. Despite being completely unaccountable to the EU electorate, the ECB jealously guards its own independence. National parliaments cannot influence ECB policy, but the bank gets to influence government policies through the Stability and Growth Pact. Under this pact, governments cannot run a deficit of more than 3 per cent on their current accounts or accumulate debts of more than 60 per cent on their yearly national income accounts (GDP). This effectively blocks governments from responding to popular pressures for increased spending on welfare or services. The ECB has a sole mandate to control inflation and, unlike the US Federal Reserve, it is not obliged to promote economic policies which reduce unemployment. It uses this exclusive mandate to restrict wage rises.

According to Onaran, the last 20 years have seen 'productivity increases exceed changes in real wages in all Western EU countries'.[40] The adjusted wage share in national income has also fallen by around 10 per cent, exposing the class biases behind the technical finery with which the ECB surrounds itself. Workers have lost everywhere but workers in the periphery have been particularly badly affected as the ECB systematically favours capital within the European core. In the words of Costas Lapavitsas, monetary union is a classical imperialist device as it transfers wealth from workers to capital *at the same time* as it transfers wealth from the periphery to the centre.[41]

Before the crash, the ECB presided over an explosion of private debt in the peripheral countries of the EU. It did this in order to help create a market for the goods of corporations based in the bigger EU industrial powers. According to Lapavitsas, more than 65 per cent of German exports make their way to other EU countries annually.[42] Having squeezed the living conditions of its own employees, German capitalism needed to offload commodities in foreign markets. So, bankers in Germany, France and Britain recycled profits as loans to these peripheral countries in order to achieve this. Despite Angela Merkel's pronouncements, governments in Greece and Portugal never engaged in a vast amount of public spending. Prior to the crisis, the restrictions in the Stability and Growth Pact largely worked to constrain public deficits, but they never restrained the borrowing of the private sector.[43] Desperate to sustain the mirage of successful integration, peripheral governments sanctioned vast amounts of borrowing by their private financial systems. By 2008 this amounted to some €1.4 trillion.

Once the crash occurred, the ECB's main purpose was to save the EU banks who churned out these loans. The only way it could do so was to make national governments responsible for private-backed debt even though this would, inevitably, lead to a crisis in government spending. The ECB then refused to directly help governments who ran up public spending deficits and used their crisis to demand 'structural reform'. The cynicism of the ECB is starkly illustrated in a 'carry-over' scam known as the Long Term Re-Financing Operation. In December 2011 and February 2012, the ECB offered unlimited financing to European banks at an interest rate of just 1 per cent for three years.

About 800 banks drew down over €1 trillion under this facility and then, with a few flicks of a computer mouse, they shifted this money into buying government bonds. At the time the interest rate on Irish, Spanish or Italian bonds was around 5.5 per cent and so that represented a neat profit of 4.5 per cent. Bloomberg's accurately described it as a 'free lunch' for the banks and estimated that it gave them an extra €120 billion in profit.[44]

Just like the IMF, the ECB has used the turmoil of the Eurozone crisis to gain crucial leverage over the economies of Europe. Structural adjustment policies have been the order of the day everywhere, with workers paying the costs to stabilise the banks and corporations.

A Fake Bailout

The Troika arrived in Ireland in late November 2010. In the weeks prior to their arrival, the cost of Irish government borrowing had skyrocketed to over 9 per cent.[45] This was not sustainable in the medium to long term, but according to officials, the state was well funded into 2011 and was not in need of external assistance.[46] The Irish elite were desperate to avoid an IMF/EU intervention because of the loss of sovereignty that this would necessitate. However, an intervention by the President of the ECB soon changed their thinking. As part of its unprecedented support for the private banks, the ECB had pumped €150 billion into the Irish financial system in return for some very dubious collateral assets. This money was provided to ensure the Irish banks could pay their debts to their British, French and German counterparts. However, the ECB started to get nervous about whether it would get its own money back. So in a series of letters to Minister for Finance Brian Lenihan, Jean-Claude Trichet demanded that Ireland seek external 'assistance' or risk the loss of ECB funding.[47] Through veiled threats, Trichet told Lenihan that the ECB was monitoring Ireland's commitment to austerity and was making its continued support contingent on spending cuts and tax increases.[48] These bully-boy tactics immediately had the desired effect. On the day he received one of the letters, Lenihan announced a €15 billion adjustment in the public finances to be implemented by 2015. Two weeks later, the government signed up to the €85 billion Troika programme designed to protect the banks and restructure the state in the interests of big business. Lenihan could have resisted ECB pressure but he knew an austerity programme also suited the corporate elite in Ireland and so he embraced it fully.

Each of the Troika institutions put up €22.5 billion, with the remaining €17.5 billion coming from the Irish Pension Reserve Fund. Framed as a 'bailout', the cost of the loan would be around 5.8 per cent or more than 3 per cent higher than the European Financial Stability Fund was able to borrow at.[49] This effectively meant the Troika would be *making money* by lending to Ireland, borrowing cheaply in international markets, before charging Ireland a hefty premium.[50] In return for this 'generosity', it also gained significant control over economic policy.

The first thing the Troika did was to forbid the Irish state from including bondholders in any form of burden sharing. This group, which includes the asset management arms of some of the richest banks in the world (BNP Paribas, Aviva, Axa Paris, Deutsche Investment and Goldman Sachs) was now totally protected.[51] The government had already committed to paying off secured (insured) bondholders, but according to the Minister for Transport, Leo Varadkar, if they sought to exclude unsecured bondholders a financial 'bomb would go off in Dublin'.[52] Speaking in more measured tones, Jörg Asmussen from the ECB Executive Board confirmed as much in April 2012:

> I know that the decisions concerning the repayment of bondholders in the former Anglo Irish Bank have been a source of controversy . . . It is true that the ECB viewed it as the least damaging course to fully honour the outstanding senior debts of Anglo. However unpopular that may now seem, this assessment was made at a time of extraordinary stresses in financial markets . . . to ensure no negative effects spilled over to other Irish banks or to banks in other European Countries. . . Therefore, the ECB remains of the opinion that Ireland should honour its commitments stemming from the promissory notes, as foreseen. This in our view is the best way to regain sustainable market access.[53]

Having 'bailed out' the bondholders, it remained to 'bail in' the taxpayers. In an extremely cynical move a government, with less than three months left in office, signed a Memorandum of Understanding with the Troika committing the state to years of austerity. This allowed the incoming administration to claim it was 'duty bound' to honour an agreement it pretended to detest. Since March 2011, the Fine Gael–Labour government has picked up where their predecessors left off, implementing a raft of structural adjustment policies in areas from taxation to labour markets and social spending. The Troika and their supporters in the Irish government are determined to 'never waste a good crisis' and are using it as pretext to change the nature of Irish society. The experiments that the IMF had developed in the 1980s to squeeze poorer countries in Latin America and Africa are now being brought to the European mainland. Unsurprisingly this means a new era of vast social suffering has dawned.

3

The Failure of Austerity

When the Irish Prime Minister, Enda Kenny, visited Berlin in October 2011, he received the red carpet treatment. There was little talk about the calamitous collapse of his country's economy. Instead *Der Spiegel* suggested that the German Prime Minister Merkel would 'be generous in her praise of her guest'.[1] She wanted an example for how austerity was working and Ireland was the good example. If Greece symbolised crisis and political instability, Ireland signified an oasis of calm in difficult times. The implication was that its people would soon reap the economic rewards for their obedience. A similar message was assiduously repeated by Irish government Ministers and at one stage, the Finance Minister, Michael Noonan, even joked that he would print T-shirts with the words 'Ireland is not Greece'.[2] Increasingly, Ireland has also been elevated to the status of 'model pupil' of the IMF and the EU Commission. Antonio Borges, the IMF's European department director, has claimed that its austerity programme was 'exemplary' and has linked it to a 'surprisingly positive' economic performance.[3] The EU Commission President, José Manuel Barroso, publicly praised Ireland's progress and staff at the Directorate General for Economic and Financial Affairs have stated that the Irish 'authorities are to be commended for continued strong programme implementation'.[4]

However, this praise is highly ideological. Its primary purpose is to point to an imaginary solution for a deep economic crisis that has enveloped the European periphery and which is spreading to its core. The stark reality behind the Irish story is that austerity is not working. Ireland's austerity policies have been underpinned by a consensus that has straddled the state, business, conventional economists and the media. At its core was a rejection of any form of Keynesian solution to the crisis. The Irish state, it was asserted, could play little role in stimulating the economy because it was a small, open country and the benefits of any stimulus package would only flow to its economic rivals. The Irish strategy would instead focus on 'regaining competitiveness' in order to gain increased market share for its exports. As the crisis developed, these arguments have hardened into a dogma even as they diverge ever more from reality. They are summarised below.

1. *As every state needs a functioning banking system, it was necessary to bail out and fully recapitalise the banks.*

At the start of the crisis in 2008, the Minister for Finance, Brian Lenihan, claimed that it would be 'the cheapest bailout in the world'[5] but unfortunately, this claim fell somewhat wide of the mark. If account is taken of potential losses in NAMA, Standard and Poor's has estimated that the total cost of Ireland's bank bailout could reach as high as €90 billion.[6] Even if we confine the figure to the direct bailout of €64 billion, it will still be one of the most expensive bailouts in world history. Stephen Donnelly, the Independent TD (Deputy to the Dail), summed it up graphically.

> That's €14,000 for every man, woman and child in Ireland. We have paid three and a half times more than each person in Iceland, four times more than each Greek, six times more than each Cypriot, 23 times more than every Portuguese, 10 times more than every Spaniard and almost 200 times more than each Italian . . . The burden which has been imposed is, literally, unbearable.[7]

2. *The Irish state can cope with this level of sovereign debt. There would be a few hard years but the finances of the state would eventually recover.*

The main advocate of this position has been the Economic and Social Research Institute (ESRI). In its *Quarterly Economic Commentary* in the Spring of 2010, it stated that the debt was 'manageable' and 'would in no way threaten the solvency of the state'.[8] A year later its chief economist, John Fitzgerald, claimed that if the Irish government stuck to its austerity programme, 'the Irish debt burden will stabilise at a manageable level in 2013 and 2014', though there would be considerable uncertainty in the future.[9] In order to honour its 'manageable' debts, the Irish government has taken €28 billion out of its economy since 2008 in a series of six harsh budgets. This is one of the biggest fiscal adjustments of any advanced country in modern times.[10]

Two measures are typically used for measuring the size of an economy. Gross Domestic Product (GDP) refers to the market value of goods and services produced in a country in a given year. Gross National Product (GNP) is also a measure of the value of goods and services but its focus is on those resident in the country. So it adds income earned from abroad, and crucially, subtracts income that is repatriated to other countries. GNP is a better measure of the real size of the Irish economy because multinationals often declare an artificially high value for the goods they produce in Ireland to minimise their taxes. They then engage in a vast repatriation of this artificial income which was never really produced here. In 2011, for example, a staggering €31 billion was taken out of the economy and so the measure of the size of the Irish economy captured by GNP was considerably lower than the GDP – €127 billion versus €159.[11] If we use GNP rather than GDP as the measure for the size of the Irish economy, the ESRI argument about 'manageable' debt falls apart. The general government debt is just over 150 per cent of GNP – and will stay like this for the foreseeable future, as Table 3.1 illustrates. These figures are based on the Department of Finance projections for economic growth and even these may be somewhat optimistic. If they are, Ireland's situation will be even worse. Currently, Ireland

Table 3.1: General Government Debt, GNP and Debt to GNP Ratio (€billion)

	2012	2013	2014	2015
GNP	130	134	138	143
General Government Debt	192	204	210	212
Debt to GNP ratio	148%	152%	152%	149%

Source: Department of Finance Medium Term Financial Statement 2012, Table 3.2 and 4.1.

comes fourth in the EU debt league – but this is when the measure used is based on GDP. If the alternative GNP measure is used, Ireland hits Greek-style debt ratios.

3. *The key to growth is for Ireland to export its way out of the recession. To do so, it has to increase competitiveness.*

The main strength of the Irish economy has been its export performance and this has led to a trade surplus during the four years of the recessions, as Table 3.2 indicates. The state's strategy is to grow these exports in order to pull the Irish economy forward, thus reducing the debt to GDP ratio.

While Ireland's trade surplus is fairly impressive, it arises primarily from a decline in imports, which reflect the calamitous fall in the domestic market. The export figures are concentrated on a very narrow spectrum which is dominated by foreign multinationals. Two-thirds of all manufactured exports are composed of chemicals, pharmaceuticals and medical service exports. Building a recovery strategy on a small number of export industries to the detriment of the domestic economy is precarious for two reasons. First, the austerity experts have been far too optimistic about the state of the global economy. They assumed that there would be a V-shaped recovery – a calamitous fall, followed by an equally spectacular rise. In fact, the stagnation in the world capitalist system persisted for far longer than they expected. Recovery in the US was, at best, sluggish while the EU moved back into recession rather than onwards to full recovery. Second, the pharmaceutical

Table 3.2: Ireland's Imports, Exports and Trade Surplus (€million)

Year	Imports	Exports	Trade Surplus
2007	63,486	89,226	25,741
2008	57,585	86,394	28,810
2009	45,061	84,239	39,178
2010	45,764	89,193	43,429
2011	48,315	91,228	42,913

Source: Central Statistics Office, Trade Statistics, August 2012.

industry, which accounts for over half of Ireland's goods exports, has entered a new stage of decline due to the 'patent cliff'. Major block-buster drugs are coming off patent and can be produced by rivals in other countries as generic drugs for a much cheaper price. In the next few years, ever more patents will expire and there is little sign of new products emerging.

4. *One of the main ways in which competitiveness could be increased was by reducing pay.*

The demand for pay cuts arose from the employers' organisation, the Irish Business and Employers' Confederation (IBEC). In February 2009, they issued a policy document which called for a 'downward correction of the order of 10 per cent' and, while acknowledging that it would have a deflationary effect in 2009 and 2010, claimed that it would lead to a bold recovery thereafter.[12] At first their call was not particularly successful and it only gained traction after the government embarked on pay cuts for its own employees. A pensions levy which averaged a 7.5 per cent cut on gross pay was imposed on the public sector in February 2009 and this was then followed in December 2009 by pay cuts of 5 per cent on the first €30,000 of salary, 7.5 per cent on the next €40,000 of salary and 10 per cent on the next €55,000.

The link between the public and private sectors was significant. Private sector employers were not strong enough by themselves to enforce pay reductions and, moreover, could face a number of legal complications in attempting to do so. But when the state cut the pay of its own staff, it set targets for private employers to follow because they were able to present pay cuts as national policy and avoid detailed examination of their own balance sheets. A major propaganda assault was mounted against public sector workers to weaken their resolve to resist. Yet figures from the OECD provided a more complex picture than the myth-makers might suggest. These showed that the salary levels of medical specialists or consultant doctors were way above the OECD average and so too were those of central government managers but that was as far as it went. Using a comparison based on purchasing power parities and adjusted for differences in hours and holidays, the average annual compensation for employees in executive secretarial positions in the public sector was just over the OECD average while the compensation for secretarial positions was just under.[13] The starting pay of teachers tended to be below the OECD average while the remuneration of those at the top of their scale is above. Irish teachers, however, have also longer class contact hours than their counterparts in other OECD countries.[14]

Despite all of this, the argument for pay cuts was given intellectual support by the ESRI Professor John Fitzgerald, who put the matter succinctly in an article entitled 'How Ireland Can Stage an Economic Recovery'. He suggested that 'if cuts in public sector pay rates mirrored cuts in private sector wage rates there would be a very significant gain in competitiveness, with a consequent big reduction in unemployment after three or four years.'[15] However, once again, this argument does not stand up to scrutiny. First, 'competitiveness' must, presumably, refer to export industries as competitors on the domestic market have a level playing field with regard to wages. Yet when we examine the industries which have been most successful at exporting, they happen to be the ones that pay the highest wages. Together, chemicals and pharmaceuticals, which account for the bulk of exports, paid an average of €19.85 an hour compared to an average of €15.11 an hour for all of manufacturing in 2007.[16] (Figures are, unfortunately, not available in later years.) One reason for the export success of these high paying sectors is that wages are just one cost that enters the wider equation of competition. Others include levels of productivity, marketing strategies, choices of products and so on. If low wages were the sole criterion for economic success, then Africa would be a booming continent. The second reason why Fitzgerald's article was wrong is that his predictions simply bear no relationship to reality. The article was written in 2009 and the big reduction in unemployment that was supposed to occur 'three or four years later' is nowhere in sight.

5. *Wage cuts would not necessarily depress the economy. They would rather increase the 'confidence' of international investors and so Ireland would benefit from being the model pupil.*

The Irish population were spun a new morality tale: if they took pain for a short number of years, they would reap rewards later. It was almost as if there had to be atonement for the party years of the Celtic Tiger and expert economic advice was on hand to show that this was a viable strategy. Thus Kevin O'Rourke, Professor of Economics at Trinity College Dublin, informed the population in a popular piece in the *Irish Independent* that 'the cross-country evidence from the Great Depression is unambiguous: the more wages fell during the 1930s, the less output declined'.[17]

The government has been largely successful at depressing the living standards of those at work. In 2009, the average annual disposable income for those at work stood at €28,732 but by 2011 this had dropped to €26,907.[18] Findings from the Fifth European Survey on Working Conditions have shown that Irish and Baltic state workers were among those most likely to have experienced a pay cut in 2010. Just under half (48 per cent) of Irish workers have experienced a pay cut compared to 16 per cent of all European workers.[19] But even though wages have been driven down, there is no sign that output is increasing. Despite the predictions about what would happen if Ireland stuck with its austerity policies, its economy declined year on year for four years. In 2007, at the height of the Celtic Tiger, Irish GNP stood at €142 billion but it has declined constantly and stood at €128 billion in 2011.[20] That represented a fall of 15 per cent and, although there was a small pick-up in 2012, it is calamitous for any society. It also shows that those who cheer led the strategy of austerity got it very wrong.

Economic Expertise and Class Bias

These dogmas formed the consensus between the Irish state and the intellectual establishment but they were barely subject to debate. Instead, they were presented as technical solutions that transcended politics and were handed down by learned experts. There was supposed to be no policy choices because there were simply no other 'realistic' solutions. Margaret Thatcher's TINA mantra – 'there is no alternative' – was repeated continually, along with its twenty-first-century version: 'We are where we are and we must live in the real world.' Economic experts appeared so frequently in the media that their omniscience created a new mythology about the cause of the crisis. 'Incompetence' by state officials was deemed to be the source of Ireland's woes and, it was implied, if only proper economic experts had been in charge, it might have been avoided. Top civil servants, apparently, 'fell asleep at the wheel' and failed to see the warning signs. According to the Wright Commission, one of the key reasons for the failure was that the Irish Department of Finance had an 'extraordinarily low' number of professional economists in its employment and it failed to have 'sufficient engagement with the broader economic community in Ireland'.[21] The solution was the creation of an 'independent' Fiscal Advisory Council composed of such experts.

The focus, however, on the expertise of elite decision makers ignores the policy bias of the Irish state towards neoliberalism. It also ignores how most professional economists championed that bias and failed to predict the massive crisis facing the Irish economy. The ESRI, for example, claimed in 2008 that there would be 'a modest recovery in 2009'; that GNP would grow by 3 per cent and that 24,000 net jobs would be created.[22] Yet despite this evident failure of analysis, professional economists have effectively been exonerated and are deemed to be more needed than ever. As Ireland turned its back on the Catholic Church and becomes more secular, conventional economists appear to have taken up the role vacated by the priesthood. The new economic priesthood read the markets rather than deities and preach their sermons from television studios rather than church pulpits. Ironically, however, the message bears a remarkable similarity. Sacrifices from the majority are necessary for the atonement of sin and the promise of a happier life in the hereafter. This elevation of economic expertise serves as a thin disguise for avoiding questions about the direction of Irish state policy after the crash. Yet all the evidence suggests that it has deepened poverty and inequality. To put it more bluntly, the reliance on expertise from neoliberal economists gives cover to a class bias.

One of the ways this bias works is by narrowing discussion on the Irish crisis to one question: how do we fix the fiscal deficit? Typically, critics of austerity are asked to explain 'How would you fix the €18 billion black hole in the economy?' and are never asked: why has there been a €30 billion fall in investment and what do you propose to do about it? Respondents are supposed to provide an answer to the first question in a few short sentences but, crucially, they must stick to the rules of the capitalist economy. In other words, they have to give an answer to a problem caused by the system without questioning the nature of the system itself. Yet the fiscal deficit is, in fact, a symptom rather than a root cause of the crisis. It was caused in the first instance by the decision to pay off private bank debt. Then as a result of austerity policies, which cut back on domestic demand, many were thrown out of work and tax revenue fell. These combined problems meant that interest payments on Irish state debt rose from €2 billion in 2008, to €4.9 billion in 2010, to €5.1 billion in 2011 and to €6.3 billion in 2012. An obvious answer to the 'black hole' problem might, therefore, be to halt the repayments of this interest and default on the bank debt that was imposed on the Irish population by the ECB. But precisely this type of response is defined as 'political ideology' and not a suitable answer to the technical, neutral question. In this manner, the restrictive nature of media discussions on the 'black hole' question sets up a parameter that dovetails with the interpretations of the political establishment.

The 'How do we fix the fiscal deficit' question was also used to de-politicise the wider austerity programme by presenting it as a form of good housekeeping. No household, it was asserted, could run up debts forever and neither could a country. This clichéd metaphor was originally used by Margaret Thatcher to justify her attack on the welfare state but her homely image does not stand the test of logic. A society is not like a household because there are different social classes within it. In a household, savings result from a voluntary co-operative effort to abstain but in society, the 'savings' extracted from one social group are the result of attacks mounted by another. In a household, the savings of today create extra holidays for tomorrow but in society the money saved in welfare cuts or lost wages is never returned. In a household, savings can be a way of accumulating funds that lead to an increase in wealth. In a society, the money 'saved' from working people simultane-ously cuts their demand and so helps push other workers out of their jobs. Concentrating, then, on 'how to get the budget right' – as if it were a matter of organising family savings, invariably produces a distorted picture.

Yet even within the narrow, ideologically prescribed limits set by the dominant media a distinct class bias is evident in the way the state has tried to close the public spending gap. This is clearly apparent in the six budgets which have been introduced since the crisis began. Discussions on these often focus on which income categories were most affected but while this is a legitimate and interesting question, it ignores a larger issue: how much extra tax is taken from *income* rather than *capital*. The majority of those who live on an income receive a wage and are Pay As You Earn (PAYE) workers. Others, who are usually more fortunate, live off dividends, rent, property, speculation or profit. As Table 3.3 shows, however, income earners carry the burden of increases in taxation. Moreover, while tax revenue has declined since the crash of 2007, its sources have become more heavily reliant on income earners. In 2007, for example, income tax accounted for 27 per cent of all revenue but by 2012 it accounted for 42 per cent when taken in conjunction with the Universal Social Charge. By contrast, corporation and capital taxes dropped from 20 per cent to 13 per cent.[23]

Ninety-five per cent of Irish income tax earners earn less than €100,000 and 55 per cent have a gross income below €30,000.[24] A strategy, therefore, of hitting income earners will predominantly affect those on low and middle incomes. They will carry a bigger burden for

Table 3.3: Additional Tax Revenue Raised in Budgets from Income and Capital, 2008–2013 (€million)

Year Tax	Revenue from Income Tax	Revenue from Capital
2008	€1,140	€63*
2009	€2,786	€147
2010	€53	€0
2011	€1,192	€275**
2012	€47	€174***
2013	€367	€123
TOTAL	€5,585	€782

Source: Department of Finance, Budget and Estimates Measures, Various Years. Figures for tax revenue on capital compiled from corporation profit tax, capital acquisitions tax and capital gains tax.

* Includes reduction in tax relief for Approved Retirement Funds (APFs).

** Includes further restrictions on tax relief for APFs and removal of some property reliefs.

*** Includes removal of some property reliefs.

solving the fiscal deficit. This elementary fact is often obscured by the claim that those earning over €100,000 pay a considerable amount of the actual income tax received. This, however, is not fully true because this claim is usually based on 'tax cases' rather than individuals. Tax cases can include married couples whose combined income is €100,000 and so figures are inflated by these middle income couples. Nevertheless, even if wealthier income earners pay a higher proportion of this overall revenue, it does not follow that poorer income earners have not borne a disproportionate burden of a crisis. Increased taxes on those who earn over €100,000 are far easier to carry than increases on those under €30,000 – even if the former are higher.

The other main area for generating tax revenues has been indirect taxes. Traditionally, Ireland has relied heavily on indirect taxes rather than taxes on wealth or capital, with 44 per cent of its overall taxation being derived from this source as compared to an average of 35 per cent for the EU.[25] The longer-term strategy of the state is to increase reliance on such taxes through carbon taxes and an increased rate of VAT. The 2010 budget introduced a carbon tax and the 2012 budget has increased the standard rate of VAT to 23 per cent. Between them, these two taxes will raise €1 billion annually. There is considerable evidence to show that indirect taxes hit the poorest sections of the population harder. One international study showed that the poorest 10 per cent pay at least twice as much indirect tax relative to their income as the richest.[26] An Irish study came to a broadly similar conclusion, suggesting that 'indirect tax payments for households in the lowest decile amounted to almost 21 per cent of income – the corresponding figure at the upper end of the distribution was 9.6 per cent'.[27]

The other strategy for closing the 'fiscal deficit' has been to cut public spending but this has also tended to hit lower income groups harder. The largest cut in the 2012 budget was on social welfare protection, with a projected €812 million in savings. These were concentrated on lone parents, the unemployed and short-time workers, the elderly and large families. Lone parents have been a particular target of the Labour Minister, Joan Burton, and henceforth, once a child reaches the age of 7, his or her parent will be deprived of One Parent Family Allowance. They will also only be allowed to earn €60 a week rather than €146 previously before their allowance is reduced.

Social welfare for the unemployed was cut in 2011; the rental supplement was cut by a further €6 a week in 2012; and job seeker's benefit was cut by three months in 2013. The fuel allowance for the elderly has been cut, even though Ireland has one of the highest rates of 'excess deaths' with an estimated 2800 passing away due to hypothermia annually.[28] Child benefit has been slashed in a systematic way, affecting poorer families in particular. Since 2008, those with one child have lost €36 a month; those with two have lost €72; and those with three have lost €145 a month.[29]

However, in a broader sense the attacks on public services have a discriminatory effect. By definition, the poor are more likely to rely exclusively on these services rather than others which require private funding. Even during the boom years, Irish public services lagged far behind the growth of the economy and middle income groups were encouraged to find private solutions to make up for its shortfalls.[30] Half the population took out private health insurance and many resorted to private grinds (tutors) for children to gain access to third level education. The cuts have exacerbated this two-tier system, though more people are being forced off private health insurance. The number of people, for example, who are on a first time waiting list for outpatient services was 385,462 at the end of 2012 – or almost a tenth of the population. Just less than a third of them will wait for over a year.[31] The situation for elderly patients who need long-stay beds is reaching crisis point as the state is slowly withdrawing from direct provision via the Health Services Executive (HSE). Table 3.4 illustrates the wider

Table 3.4: Beds by Category of Long Stay Accommodation

Year	HSE Extended Care	HSE Welfare Home	Voluntary Home or Hospital	Voluntary Welfare Home	Private Nursing Home	Total
2004	6135	1280	2954	N/A	9042	19,411
2006	5206	1406	1496	320	13,285	21,713
2008	5246	844	1557	378	14,932	22,967
2010	4498	715	1600	176	13,785	20,784
2011	4366	789	1773	294	13,375	20,597

Source: Department of Health, Long Stay Activity, Various Years.

pattern on closure of public beds and the growth of the private sector. One result is that 1,100 older people, who are medically in need of a nursing home place and have been through a rigorous means test, are languishing on a waiting list. They are literally waiting for others to die before accessing a bed.

Inequality and Investment

Debates in the mainstream media about how to close the fiscal deficit have been framed as one about raising extra taxes or cutting public spending. Those for raising more taxes are said to lean on the 'left' and those who favour more cuts are said to lean to the 'right'. In reality, they are both different elements of the same strategy. The low and middle income sectors of the population are carrying the burden of paying for a banking crisis that was caused by a very small elite group. There has been no serious attempt to impose a wealth tax or to increase the very low rate of corporation profits tax. The result of these policies has been a rise in social deprivation and inequality.

The deprivation rate – which is defined as those experiencing two or more types of enforced deprivation according to a common EU index – has nearly doubled from 11.8 per cent of the population in 2007 to 22.5 per cent in 2010.[32] The most significant increase was among children aged between 0 and 17 where there was a rise from 24 per cent in 2009 to 30 per cent in 2010. Average household income has also dropped 5 per cent between 2009 and 2010.[33] These figures are particularly worrying because the Irish entered the recession with one of the highest ratios of debt to disposable income in the EU. In 1995, just before the Celtic Tiger began, the ratio of household debt to disposable income stood at 48 per cent but by 2008, this had risen to 176 per cent – an increase of 267 per cent.[34]

This pattern of social suffering has also been accompanied by a rising level of inequality. Contrary to official propaganda, not everyone is 'tightening their belt'. After the crash of 2007, the net financial assets of households fell dramatically but since then they have recovered and surpassed the pre-crisis level. In 2007, the net financial assets stood at €102 billion but by the following year they had dropped to €67 billion. By 2011, however, they had increased to €120 billion representing a recovery of €53 billion on their low point.[35] This growth was so spectacular that it overtook holdings of these assets at the high point of the Celtic Tiger boom. It gave lie to the much vaunted claim that 'there was no wealth in the country'. The distribution of these assets is profoundly uneven and little research is available on its distribution. The main source of information on wealth comes from the Bank of Ireland Wealth report which was taken at the height of the boom. This indicated that the top 1 per cent of Irish society held 34 per cent of the wealth, when housing is excluded.[36] We may safely assume that the top 1 per cent continue to hold the same proportion of financial assets – which includes cash, shares, pension and insurance funds and business assets – and so have escaped much suffering.

Profits are also showing signs of recovery as a direct result of wage cuts. The dry language of the Central Statistics Office (CSO) makes the point with devastating accuracy.

> The operating surplus or profits of non-financial corporations (NFCs) increased from €35.2bn in 2009 to €37.8bn in 2010 . . . The other main component of value added is compensation of employees or wages and salaries which declined from €37.3bn in 2009 to €34.9bn in 2010. Therefore, the improved profit share relates more to a decline in payroll costs for these corporations rather than to an increase in overall value added.[37]

The following year, the CSO noted another steady rise in profits, bringing NFC profits to €46.3 billion.[38] This is quite a staggering increase and represents nearly a full recovery to where they were before the recession.

Some might argue that an increased level of inequality – particularly if it is a temporary phenomenon – might be an unpalatable but necessary feature of a recovery. From this viewpoint, the crash may simply represent an adjustment in the relative strengths between labour and capital. The redistribution in favour of profit might encourage investment and help restore confidence in the economy but once again there is little evidence to show that. All indications are that the level of investment by private corporations has shown a calamitous fall and has

Table 3.5: Gross Domestic Fixed Capital Formation (€million)

Year	Amount
2006	48,311
2007	48,377
2008	39,324
2009	25,601
2010	18,745
2011	16,112

Source: CSO, Quarterly National Accounts, *2012, Table 2.*

fallen from €48 billion to €16 billion. In the period since 2007, the investment rate fell from a high of 18 per cent in 2005 to just 8 per cent in 2011.[39] Table 3.5 illustrates the same pattern in absolute figures.

With investment declining, household consumption reducing and cuts in government spending increasing, it is difficult to see how the Irish economy can fully recover. The harsh truth is that the Irish elite gambled everything on being the model pupils of the Troika, and that gamble is coming unstuck. It thought that foreign markets and foreign investors would come to its rescue and that it could pay off a 'manageable' debt. It assumed that it could attack living standards and be pulled out of recession by multinational firms. It did everything it could to give confidence to the financial markets and so went out of its way to distance itself from Greece. Yet the difference is only one of degree. Ireland's descent has been slow, systematic and depressing while Greece's has been turbulent and dramatic. There is clearly an Irish tragedy as well as the better known Greek one.

4

The Reconfiguration
of Ireland

Rahm Emanuel, the former Chief of Staff to Barack Obama, had a piece of advice for elites: 'You never want a serious crisis to go to waste. And what I mean by that is an opportunity to do things you think you could never do before.'[1] The writer Naomi Klein named this approach the 'shock doctrine'.[2] Both were referring to the pattern whereby elites move decisively during a crisis to impose new ways of ruling. Some of these strategies may have been viewed as 'extreme' or 'off the wall' in a previous era but crises create the conditions for change. The dynamics behind this pattern are easy to understand. A natural disaster like Hurricane Katrina or a sudden economic collapse, such as the fall of the Celtic Tiger, disorientates people. The normal ways of understanding the world are shattered and people are paralysed with fear. Elites may suffer from some of these feelings but, as a group, they are more cohesive and, moreover, the privilege of ruling allows them to think in strategic terms. While others scramble to survive, elites strategise about how best to exit a crisis – on their terms.

This technique of using an economic crisis to change relationships of domination is very much in evidence in Ireland. The elite are determined to reconfigure Irish society and regard change as essential for their long-run survival. We shall examine five ways they are seeking to transform Ireland in the white heat of a crisis.

Tax Your Home

Despite a recent drop, Ireland has a very high rate of home ownership, with 70 per cent of people owning their own homes.[3] The political elite encouraged this trend by progressively reducing the stock of social housing. But from July 2013, they are imposing a property tax so that people will pay an average of between €300 and €400 a year, just to live in their own home. The government claims that this measure is necessary to broaden the tax base and to ensure a steady stream of revenue to the state. They point to the over-reliance on 'transaction taxes' which occurred during the Celtic Tiger boom when 14 per cent of monthly exchequer income came from stamp duty.[4] By introducing an annual recurring property tax, the state will be guaranteed an income stream of €500 million a year.

But why does the state have to levy the majority of the population to 'broaden the tax base'? Could there not be extra taxes on profits or dividends or financial speculation to achieve the same objective? In response, defenders of the property tax often revert to the OECD tax pyramid for support. The OECD argues that:

> income taxes seem to be associated with significantly lower levels of GDP per capita than the use of taxes on consumption and property . . . In fact, corporate income taxes appear to be the least attractive choice from the perspective of raising GDP per capita . . . it is property taxes, and particularly recurrent taxes on immovable property, that appear to be associated with the highest levels of GDP per capita.[5]

This argument conflates different classes so that they appear to share a common interest. Property taxes, it is implied, help to shift invest-ment to the productive sector and so workers and employers gain.

The proposal for a property tax has also been given a more progressive veneer by the TASC think-tank. It claimed that a property tax could be devised in an 'equality-proofed' fashion and would enhance local democracy.[6] The Irish Congress of Trade Unions has adopted a similar view and has discouraged opposition to the tax. None of these arguments, however, stand up to scrutiny.

Advocates of a property tax point to two issues as evidence of its supposedly progressive nature. Namely, that there is a surcharge on properties valued at over €1 million and that the tax increases with the value of the house. However, less than 2 per cent of the revenue will be derived from properties valued at over €1 million meaning the vast majority of the taxes will be raised from homes which are not 'trophy' units.[7] The use of the concept of 'market value' also means that the tax on a smaller house in Dublin will be higher than a mansion in Mayo. Moreover, the tax is only levied on the first acre of the property and not the rest. This is particularly beneficial to wealthy individuals like the Health Minister, James Reilly, who owns the 12-bedroomed Laughton House, situated on 150 acres of Offaly soil. He will be charged a property tax on just one of those acres while the other 149 will be exempt. When this was pointed out the Fine Gael leader, Enda Kenny, replied, 'The deputy is entitled, given that Ireland is a country in which there is plenty of land, to have space to stand outside his house and stand back to see if it is painted properly.'[8]

Even more ominously, there is not necessarily a relationship between the market value of houses and ability to pay. People may inherit a home but have limited incomes. Or they can live in an area that has a high market value and be unemployed. In other words, owning a high value property does not imply you can pay high annually recurring taxes. The original proposal for a property tax from the Commission on Taxation made some attempt to deal with situations where people had a low income but owned a family home. It suggested 'a general waiver exempting house-owners under a low income threshold' and that this should be linked to long-term social welfare rates and the annualised minimum income.[9] It further proposed special taxes on zoned development land to pay for these exemptions. Yet neither of these suggestions was taken up.

The hollowness of the progressive rhetoric is evident in the decision to tax 125,000 local authority tenants – despite recommendations to the contrary from both the Commission on Taxation and the Interdepartmental Review Group.[10] Local authority tenants do not own property yet the government is making them subject to a 'property' tax. This shows that the primary purpose is not taxing an asset which can be traded to accumulate wealth. The aim is to levy the majority of the population – rather than the tiny financial elite who caused the economic crisis.

The OECD's argument about a link between economic growth and property taxes is also entirely specious. It takes no account of wider economic policies or the particular advantages that a country historically inherited. It makes even less sense in the Irish context because €28 billion has already been taken out of the Irish economy in tax hikes and public spending cutbacks. Targeting the spending power of the vast majority through a further €500 million annual levy can only lead to a greater decline in the domestic economy. Moreover, as Keynesian economists have long pointed out, those on lower and middle incomes are more likely to spend within the domestic economy than the wealthier sections.

If the state's concern was to both grow the economy and ensure a steady stream of revenue, it would introduce a wealth tax rather than a home tax. A wealth tax might target assets that are valued at over €1 million and would not be focused on the majority of family homes. While the value of property assets has fallen considerably, the value of other financial assets have risen over recent years and there is now a 50–50 split between property and financial assets. A wealth and assets register is required to accurately gauge its distribution. But it is already clear that a wealth tax of between 2 and 5 per cent would raise as much as the property tax and ensure a steady stream of revenue.

The argument that a property tax will help local democracy makes even less sense. The central funding for local government has been cut by 20 per cent between 2008 and 2012. This funding is made up primarily of a General Purpose Grant and Government Grants and Subsidies. Table 4.1 illustrates how both have been cut by €522 million – which just happens to be the approximate figure the government hopes will be raised from the property tax. In other words, property taxes will not lead to any improvement in local authority services or extra revenue streams. It will simply facilitate the diversion of money that previously went to local government into bondholders' pockets.

The argument about improving local democracy rests entirely on the claim that local authorities can vary the charge by 15 per cent. If they reduce the charge, they will have to make do with less libraries, parks or road maintenance. If they increase it, they have extra funds to

Table 4.1: Central Government Grants to Local Authorities, 2008–2012

Year	General Purpose Grant (€m)	Government Grants and Subsidies (€m)	Total (€m)
2008	1,000	1,192	2,192
2009	937	1,255	2,192
2010	773	1,105	1,878
2011	705	1,129	1,834
2012	651	959	1,670

Source: Local Authority Revenue Account Summary 2001–2012, in Department of Environment, Community and Local Government Local Authority Budgets 2012.

play with. In other words, the parameters are set and local councillors get to choose between cuts and extra levies. This type of decision making is precisely what neoliberals prefer as it diverts the debate away from overall funds into one about the respective merits of the hangman's noose or the firing squad.

The state, however, has by no means relied on intellectual arguments to promote the property tax. Instead it has rushed through Local Property Tax legislation to give Revenue draconian powers of collection. Article 12 states that 'the Revenue Commissioners shall not be required firstly to inquire into the ownership of, or title to, any particular residential property'.[11] In other words, they do not have to show legal proof that people actually own a property. All they need to do is make an 'inference'. Article 42 deals with a situation where two people own a property but are separated. It states that if a return is made, it shall 'bind the other liable person'.[12] Article 46 imposes a fine of €1000 for those who do not disclose information on homeowners, when they have been served with a notice by Revenue Commissioners. Article 65 gives the Revenue Commissioners powers to deduct the property tax from a worker's wage. It also absolves the Revenue Commissioners of any requirement of confidentiality so that they can tell employers exactly what their employees own. Article 84 allows the Minister of Social Protection to deduct the property tax from social welfare recipients, while Article 102 allows the Revenue to get deductions from agricultural payments to farmers. Article 146 states that failure to make a return of the self-assessment form can be punished by a penalty that is equivalent of the property tax that should be paid. So if the property tax was supposed to be €405, the person would be liable for an additional penalty of the same amount, i.e. €810 in total.

These draconian measures became necessary because the government did not receive any mandate from the electorate for a property tax. In fact they were elected on the very opposite commitments. The Fine Gael manifesto stated that 'a recurring, residential property tax on the family home is unfair' and promised alternative measures to fund local authorities.[13] The Labour Party favoured a 'site value charge' that implied a tax on the value of the land, regardless of the building on it. It also stated that there should be exemptions for those who recently paid large sums in stamp duty and those in negative equity.[14] However, the Labour Party neither got a site value tax or its proposed exemptions.

In a situation where a government imposes another austerity tax without any mandate, the only available option to people is civil disobedience. The slogan of the American Revolution – No Taxation without Representation – has, it appears, a particular poignancy in twenty-first-century Ireland. Indeed, the manner in which the tax is being gathered almost invites civil disobedience. The Irish property tax is based, unusually, on a form of self-assessment and the main reason is that the state does not have the administrative capacity to gather the tax – without a large degree of public compliance. The Thornhill commission, which was charged with the design of a property tax, acknowledged that the state lacked a 'comprehensive database of residential properties (which would include information on location, property size and values of recent transactions and rental incomes)'[15] and that this represented a 'challenge' in implementation.[16] It also acknowledged that when people filled in forms to pay the €100 household charge – which preceded the property tax – this formed a 'major element of the necessary database to apply a property tax'.[17] However, as large numbers of homeowners refused to fill in these forms, the database has many holes. Moreover, the state is in a far weaker position to establish 'market value' of homes when there are few houses being sold. It, therefore, needs people to be compliant and relies on the fear of the Revenue Commissioners to enforce its will.

Pay for Your Water

In the mid 1990s, the Irish government tried to make people pay for water. It provoked enormous outrage and a campaign of civil disobedience. When contractors entered the Hillview housing estate in Waterford city, for example, to turn off the water supply of non-payers, they were surrounded with hundreds of protestors and driven away. In other areas, teams of plumbers associated with the anti-water charges movement reconnected those who had been disconnected. Eventually, in 1997 the government relented and water charges for domestic users were abolished – much to the chagrin of the neoliberal elite in both Ireland and the EU. The economic crash has, however, given them an opportunity to revisit the issue.

Ireland is renowned as a wet country with twice the annual rainfall as a country like Spain. Almost 82 per cent of its water supply comes from surface rain[18] and, while this is not cost-free, it suggests that there is no scarcity of water. Until very recently, there had been a systematic underspending on the infrastructure necessary to bring water to people's homes. Even official reports acknowledge that there is a backlog of required investment in essential projects of approximately €500 million.[19] Yet instead of rectifying this with a massive investment programme – and simultaneously creating jobs – the state is proposing to reduce its investment in water supply. Between 2011 and 2014, the state will cut its investment from €435 million to €296 million – a reduction of 32 per cent.[20] In agreement with the Troika, it is moving towards 'full-cost recovery in the provision of water services'.[21] Or, in simpler English, making citizens pay for their water.

The primary justification for this is water conservation. If the state's rhetoric was a crude 'we-want-you-to-pay-more-charges' it would garner little support. But when it asserts that charges are necessary to conserve a valuable resource, it takes the moral high ground and creates a 'watch thy neighbour' atmosphere. Delinquent individuals who let their taps run or take too many showers have been constructed as the primary culprits in water waste. This reflects a more general pattern where neoliberal arguments about 'user fees' are dressed up in green colours so that an apparently moral dimension is added to bill paying. Through this rhetoric, the problem of water waste is individualised and the solution is seen as universal metering to make conservation necessary.

However, the problem of water wastage in Ireland is not primarily caused by individuals. Two-fifths of Irish water is unaccounted for because of leaks from the piping system.[22] This is twice the OECD average and is a direct result of the state's failure to update the piping system. Universal metering – even if it were possible – would not solve the problem and is a costly way of diverting much needed resources away from investment in infrastructure. Countries with the highest level of metering are, ironically, often those with the highest level of water consumption. In Canada, for example, 61 per cent of households are metered yet consumption per capita is 300 litres a day. In the US, where metering is nearly universal, consumption is 425 litres per person per day.[23] In Ireland, by contrast, where water is free, the consumption is 150 litres per person per day – half the Canadian rate and a third that of the US.

It might, however, be argued that these differences reflect wider cultural patterns and that we should instead examine how metering can change patterns of usage within individual countries. This has, in fact, been examined for the past 30 years in Britain and the evidence is highly tenuous. Water metering trials were established in the Isle of Wight for 53,000 households between 1989 and 1993 to test this link. They showed that compulsory metering was associated with an 11 per cent reduction in water consumption. However, 40 per cent of this reduction arose from better detection of leaks rather than more disciplined water consumption.[24] Moreover, the conservation effects wore off after a period of time and therefore, it might be assumed, that the public education campaign associated with the project had a bigger effect than the meters.

Even if we accept the claim made in the more recent Walker report in Britain that metering is linked to a reduction of 15 litres per person per day in consumption[25] – and, as we have seen, extraneous factors can enter into the equation – then further queries arise. In Ireland, the cost of metering will range between €500 million and €1 billion and it is more likely to be on the higher side as the state is using smart meters in order to make reading easier and defeat opposition. Metering and subsequent billing will also require high, recurring administrative costs. We might, therefore, ask if this is the most effective way of ensuring conservation or are there alternative ways of using the money? Alternatives might include state investment, public education and home insulation. The money spent on metering, for example, could be invested in improving the infrastructure so that wastage of water is cut to at least the average OECD level. A major, ongoing public education programme would also contribute to a reduction in water wastage. However, the key strategy in water conservation should be to make a distinction between drinking water and other forms of water such as wastewater and rainwater. Drinking water is considerably more costly as great care needs to be taken with human health. Currently, 3 per cent of household water consumption is used in drinking; 28 per cent is used by toilets; 32 per cent in baths and showers; and 34 per cent in dishwashers, sinks and washing machines.[26] If a way could be found to separate drinking water from some or all of the other categories then great strides could be made in conservation.

Fortunately, this is perfectly possible through a variety of mechanisms. Rainwater can be harvested and used for non-potable purposes such as toilets or gardens. Dual flush and low flow toilets, push button sink taps, and flow diffusers might all be introduced into the building stock. A dual flush retro fit, for example, which uses 4.5 litres of water – rather than 6 litres – could save a family of three 13 litres a day. Replacing taps and shower heads with more efficient dispensers might save even more. Both these measures alone are far more cost-effective than meters.[27] If the state were really concerned about water conservation, it would grant aid such conversions and require all commercial buildings to install them. All future building regulations should also require their use.

However, conservation is only the rhetorical wrapping for an entirely different agenda on water charges. The government has established a new entity, Irish Water, to take responsibility from the 34 local authorities who previously undertook the supply of water. Irish Water is known as a 'Public Utility Model' and its primary purpose is to lay the ground for a more sophisticated form of privatisation. It builds on wider international experience where outright privatisation of water is increasingly regarded a failure, with many countries being forced to take water back into public control. Irish Water creates a framework for greater private capitalist involvement in the supply of water while absolving them of direct responsibility for collection of user fees.

Irish Water will be 51 per cent state owned and the rest of its shareholding will be drawn from private funds. The primary purpose for centralising water supply into one organisation is to create a 'self-funding' entity that is increasingly reliant on user fees and external funding. According to the architects of the strategy, PricewaterhouseCoopers, 'The public utility model is the most attractive proposition to lenders and is understood by investors who lend to water sectors in other countries'.[28] Irish Water will be run as a commercial concern, with shareholders seeking maximum returns and external lenders demanding commercial interest rates. As the state's aim is to withdraw from funding after 2018, the company will be increasingly reliant on public–private partnerships (PPP) for longer-term investment programmes. Yet PPP projects, which involve the state in signing contracts with private companies, are much more costly for taxpayers in the longer term. They also lack transparency and lock the state into a dependency relationship with corporations.[29] The relationship between the state and these corporations is covered by rules of commercial secrecy and not even the contracts are made available to the public to inspect.

The real agenda behind water charges, therefore, is not conservation but creating more opportunities for profit and diverting state spending away from public services.

Sell Off Your Forests

After Bertie Ahern stepped down as Taoiseach, he predictably sought positions in the corporate world but some were surprised when he emerged as the chairperson of the International Forestry Fund – a joint venture between a Swiss financial company Helvetia Wealth and IFS, a Dublin-based forestry assets management company. Forestry is not often seen as a great source of wealth due to the long periods that trees take to mature but global capital is nothing if not creative and over the past decade there has been a major shift of investment into land and forests. Since 2001, for example, forests and land equivalent to the size of Western Europe has been sold off to global corporations.[30] Even before the crash, Ireland had joined in this new land grab as over half the Irish forests fell into private hands. The Irish Forestry Fund – a series of investment vehicles driven by IFS – has boasted tax-free returns of 82.77 per cent over a ten-year period. However, the investment was quite modest until a new major opportunity presented itself. It began with the entry of the Troika into Irish public life. A Memorandum of Economic and Fiscal Policies which was part of the agreement with the Troika committed the Irish government to 'setting appropriate targets for the possible privatisation of state-owned assets'.[31] It was the classic neoliberal demand that accompanied structural adjustment programmes pioneered by the World Bank and the IMF in many parts of the developing world. The Irish state picked up on the signal and appointed a right-wing economist, Colm McCarthy, to do a review of state-owned companies. He had previously drawn up a report for National Toll Roads defending exorbitant charges on drivers and described part of the public sector as 'a parallel universe, suspended in space somewhere'.[32] So it came as little surprise when he recommended another wave of privatisation. Shortly afterwards, the IMF came back again and began to demand the sell-off of €5 billion of state assets.[33]

One of those assets is Coillte, the forestry company, valued at €1.2 billion. McCarthy recommended that Ireland follow the New Zealand model and sell off the harvesting rights to the trees on long-term leases.[34] To make the sell-off more attractive, he also recommended that the legal requirement to reforest be removed as it was 'unjustified and counter-productive'.[35] The government is in agreement with these suggestions and was preparing to sell off harvesting rights for 50 to 80 years' duration. It engaged in a public relations spin to suggest this is not 'real privatisation' as the land underneath the trees remains in public ownership. However, large-scale mass opposition forced a temporary retreat – although the threat remains.

Even on a narrow economic basis, privatisation makes little sense. Coillte is composed of three divisions: Forests, Panel Products and Enterprise, which develop business opportunities in areas like wind energy. It is an integrated network so that wood, for example, flows at constant prices to the panel products divisions. The panel board mills and sawmills employ 1800 and pay wages and salaries amounting to €90 million a year. A private for profit company would be under no obligation to supply this division and certainly not at non-market prices. Similarly, there would be no necessary link between tree cutting and the creation of wind farms in a privatised firm. More broadly, Coillte is a profitable state enterprise with recorded annual profits of €256 million and has eliminated the need for exchequer funding.[36]

However, the issue of forestry goes much deeper than simply economics. Coillte controls 7 per cent of the land mass of Ireland and operates an open access policy. By contrast, private forests normally engage in more clear-felling and tend to deny access. As Ireland has no tradition of rights of way over private land, the 18 million forest visits that occur each year would be in danger. The government might, of course, make some concessions to this open access sentiment in order to push through privatisation. Private owners, however, would demand a state subsidy for an acceptance of this right. Considerable resources would also be required to police this right and ensure that forests are not closed off for spurious reasons. In New Zealand, for example, private owners established their own guidelines on restrictions for conservation, fire prevention and safety which tended to be less liberal and there is no universal right to access.

Forests also create 'public goods' which private companies have no interest in. Coillte builds forest roads, maintains forest parks and spends approximately €8.5 million a year on these amenity programmes. A state forestry company can be directed to grow non-commercial trees which fit more naturally with the surrounding environment – although, unfortunately, Coillte has been somewhat remiss in this. The state is not so driven by a demand for short-term returns and, therefore, can engage in extensive reforestation, whereas private companies will not. The McCarthy proposal to remove a legal obligation to reforest is particularly ominous as forests are also a vital resource for carbon sequestration. Trees can absorb high levels of carbon and, therefore a requirement to reforest and extend the amount of land under cultivation is vital.

All of these factors explain why the scale of what is being attempted in Ireland is so unusual. In almost all countries, the state is the largest forestry owner. Even in New Zealand – which the McCarthy commission held up as a model – the state remains by far the largest owner because the privatisation only affects non-indigenous forest plantations. Unfortunately, this neat division between indigenous and non-indigenous plantation would not apply in Ireland because Coillte – as part of its commercialisation policy – has concentrated on planting non-indigenous conifers. In Sweden, the policy of selling off forests was reversed in 2001 as the state reacquired most forests. Only Chile under Pinochet and, more latterly, South Africa have pursued extensive forest privatisation. In the former case it led to considerable under-investment and many environmental problems.

In Britain, plans to privatise the public forest estate were dropped after a huge outcry. When the government established an expert group on the subject, it was confronted with a vast array of evidence to sustain the case for public ownership. For example, the expert group claimed that 'International evidence confirms that access to trees and the natural environment helps tackle mental ill-health. It improves childhood fitness, and evidence shows that people living in areas with high levels of greenery are 40 per cent less likely to be overweight or obese.'[37] The expert group rejected privatisation because 'the public forest estate contains some of our most valuable habitats and species, many of which are of international importance'.[38] It pointed to the future potential of forests in developing a green economy, claiming that 'forests have the potential to provide more low carbon material for construction and other goods, to be an alternative to fossil fuels, and to reduce our current dependency on imports.'[39] All of these arguments are equally applicable to Ireland.

Discriminate Against the Young

Immediately after the crisis began, the state inscribed forms of discrimination against the young into its routine practices. It began with social welfare when different rates of payment were established based on age. The current maximum Job Seeker's Allowance rate is €188 a week for those aged over 25 but for those aged under 21, it is only €100 and for those aged between 22 and 24, it is €144. This age-related discrimination applies whether or not a young person is living with their parents. It creates a Catch-22 situation because few people under 21 could afford to live independently on an income of €100 a week. But if they fail to move out of their parents' home, their parents' income will be taken into account in a means test and many will receive no allowance. The only solution to this dilemma is often to emigrate – and cynics might say that this is probably the intention behind this measure.

In a remarkably short period of time, the pattern of mass emigration has returned. Traditionally emigration took the youngest, most energetic and most discontented from Ireland. And it is exactly the same again – almost as if the Celtic Tiger was no more than a brief period of fantasy. A survey conducted by the National Youth Council in 2010, for example, found that 70 per cent of young people were more – rather than less – likely to emigrate in the next year.[40] But far from this simply being an atavistic cultural reflex, the resumption of mass youth emigration is linked to a state policy of age discrimination.

Once the principle of differential social welfare payments was established, it did not take long to apply different pay rates for doing the same work. The most dramatic example has occurred among nurses. Nurses who entered their profession in February 2009 were placed on the second point of their scale and received a starting salary of €33,470 which was on a par with others who had been recruited before them. Two years later, however, the state announced a general reduction of 10 per cent in the starting salaries of all public servants and this was on top of more general pay cuts. It meant that nurses, who began their career after January 2011, received a starting salary of €28,639 a year. A year later, the salary was reduced again to €27,211 as they were started on the first point of the pay scale. Then in December 2012, the Health Services Executive (HSE) announced that they were reducing the number of agency staff and in their place creating 1000 'new' jobs. These positions, however, were to receive 80 per cent of the already reduced pay scale, making a new starting salary of €22,000 per year. So nurses who began their career just four years after 2009 experienced a pay cut of 34 per cent – even though they were required to do the exact same work.

While nurses offer the most dramatic of these discriminatory pay policies, they are not alone. New entrants to teaching, for example, have experienced a loss of qualification allowances even though these continue to be paid to staff that were recruited a short few years before them. On average a newly qualified teacher will spend eight years in temporary and contract employment before getting a permanent post. But after this long, insecure wait, they will start on a lower salary and with fewer allowances and be forced to take on more supervision duties. However, there are even more dramatic forms of discrimination occurring in the area of pension provision. Younger people will be forced to work for an extra number of years as the standard retirement age of 65 has been eroded. Those born between 1955 and 1960 will not receive state pensions until they are 67 while those born after 1960 will not receive one until they are 68. The eventual aim of the state is to raise the pension age to 70. The recent single pension scheme in the public sector, for example, sets a maximum retirement age of 70 and as the current generation grows older they will find that their retirement age slips further to that date.

Although the young will work longer, they will still receive a lower pension income. Despite living in a highly productive economy, pension poverty will become a frightening prospect for the next generation. And once again the state has led the way in discriminatory practices that set a headline for the whole of society. The previous generation of public sector employees received a pension based on their final salary. If they had worked 40 years, they received half that final year salary for the rest of their lives. Newer and mainly younger employees, however, have been moved to a 'career average' scheme whereby their pension is based on the average of their pay levels throughout their career. Account is taken of the fact that the nominal salary paid at the start of the career is eroded through inflation and is accordingly adjusted with reference to the Consumer Price Index. But clearly a pension based on an average over a whole career will be less than one based on the final salary. In the private sector, these attacks on the younger generation are mirrored by the closure of defined benefit schemes for new entrants. These schemes gave a guaranteed pension based on a final salary. The new defined contribution schemes, by contrast, place the onus of risk on the employee as their pension pot is speculated on the global financial markets and they take what accrues in terms of gains or losses.

These overall discriminatory practices against the young have a number of damaging effects – and are designed precisely for this. They seek to lower aspirations and reduce the legitimate expectations of young people. The cuts in pay and social welfare, for example, along with the growth in job insecurity will help acclimatise a new generation to lower living standards. Expectations that a college education might lead to a moderate wage and a degree of comfort are simply being dashed. The discriminatory policies also create a tremendous potential for division in the workforce. Unions are increasingly seen as having accepted social peace by protecting existing members and displaying little solidarity with younger workers. It is difficult to accept, for example, that union negotiators who signed up to clauses in the Croke Park agreement protecting the wages of *'serving'* staff did not know that this was an invitation to attack new staff.[41]

Work for Your Dole

Social welfare was designed originally as a safety net to prevent those out of work falling into absolute poverty but, increasingly, organisations like the OECD view these supports as a 'rigidity' that prevents wages falling to their natural level. They want social welfare to be limited to a short time frame and desire to replace the voluntary element with greater forms of compulsion. Their ethos is being adopted enthusiastically by the Irish state and the crisis is being used to reformulate the whole concept of social welfare. Using the banal cliché of 'labour activation', a host of mechanisms have been set up to drive the long-term unemployed off social welfare.

The policy targets of the Irish government are outlined in 'Pathways to Work' and there it is stated that:

> The Department of Social Protection will engage with each person who becomes unemployed in the future with a view to reducing the average time spent on the Live Register from 21 months today to less than 12 months by the end of 2015.[42]

If this objective was to be met by a stimulus programme that created actual jobs, it would be laudable. Yet the Irish state has explicitly refused to engage in any direct job creation programme. Even if this objective was to be achieved by a development of the existing Back to Education Allowance programme it would be commendable. The Back to Education Allowance has become a significant way in which non-standard students have accessed third level education and so increased their chances on the jobs markets. Unfortunately, neither is what the Department of Social Protection has in mind.

Labour activation starts with a 'mutual obligations' approach where the recipient of social welfare is asked to sign a contract to indicate that they are actively seeking work. A Probability of Exit (PEX) profile is drawn up and those with a 'low PEX rating' have intensive interviews with an employment services advisor and 'may be directed to particular work experience and training programmes'.[43] One of these schemes is the Tus programme, which had 5000 participants in 2012. Participants in Tus are selected randomly from the live register and sanctions apply to people who refuse to take up the work scheme. They are expected to work for 19.5 hours per week and receive a payment of just €20 on top of the Job Seeker's Allowance. Work is with local community or voluntary organisations and training is not necessarily provided.

This approach is in marked contrast to the early 1990s when various schemes for community employment arose. The best known, Community Employment Scheme, was still employing 23,000 in 2012 while Jobs Initiative – which recruited those who were more than five years on the live register – employed 1281. These schemes took on vital community support projects and filled an important gap in the provision of public services. They provided a training allowance and the schemes were reasonably resourced by grant funding. However, the government has begun to dismantle some of these schemes by cutting back on training allowances and reconfiguring them. Picking up on advice from the OECD, it now asserts that Community Employment (CE) schemes ' must be temporary and should not become a disguised form of subsidised permanent employment'.[44] The duration of employment on a CE is increasingly limited to one year and there is a strategy to integrate CE schemes with the more compulsory Tus schemes.

A similar pattern is evident with the Back to Education Allowance schemes which currently provide places for 26,000 participants. The government is seemingly dissatisfied with the way the scheme functions as a tool for 'labour activation'. In a review of the Back to Education Allowance, it asserts that 'training rather than "work first" can have negative effects on return to employment because of "lock-in effects"'.[45] 'Lock-in effects' is a strange bureaucratic way to describe a phenomenon whereby students become enthusiastic about learning and seek to complete courses and, maybe, even progress further. As courses in universities normally last three years, this constitutes a 'lock-in' and so the Department of Social Protection's solution is more 'short term, full time and certain accelerated courses providing education in areas where labour shortages exist'.[46] It also wishes to move to a situation with people being referred to 'courses where job opportunities exist' rather than making a self-selection.[47] In other words, instead of the unemployed receiving an opportunity for genuine second chance education, courses are to be chosen for them according to the immediate needs of employers. Rather than a general social science degree, for example, they would be put into short-term IT courses, where employers might have an input in its design.

More worryingly, labour activation is being used to create new opportunities for profit. SOLAS is the new state agency which is supposed to replace the older scandal-ridden training agency, FAS, but its functions are more limited. It will oversee new Education Training Boards which will put out tenders for training. Private sector companies as well as state agencies such as Vocational Education Committees (VECs) will tender to provide these courses. The private companies will compete by cutting costs – often through hiring temporary teachers on lower rates. Measurements of educational 'outputs' will also be put in place to set up an artificial competitive market that will benefit private companies. The courses are also supposed to be closely aligned with the immediate needs of employers and less emphasis will be placed on genuine education – the realising of the full potential of the individual.

Labour activation strategies are primarily about pressurising the unemployed to take up poorly paid posts in Ireland's limited jobs market. They are about reducing expectations by deploying compulsion to get people to accept jobs for which they might otherwise think they are unsuitable. This element of compulsion is also designed to ensure more compliant workers. After all, people are far less likely to challenge or defy supervisors when the threat of disciplinary action entails loss of social welfare as well as sacking.

Another strategy designed to develop an ethos of compliance is the new vogue for 'internships'. These were pioneered in the US where 10 million students a year are pushed towards internships – often by their own universities.[48] The Irish state is now encouraging this practice and is currently paying €50 a week on top of social welfare for approximately 5000 graduates to undertake internships. Under this JobBridge scheme, employers are not obliged to pay any additional wages. Nor is the intern deemed to be an employee and so they are not covered by any employment protection legislation. This legal immunity provides a virtual invitation for abuse and there is increasing evidence that this is occurring. The giant company Tesco, for example, sought to recruit 200 Christmas staff in 2012 under the guise of providing internships. The Chartered Accountants of Ireland selected administrative support staff for redundancies – while taking on interns to do similar work. In an extraordinary coincidence, all of those selected by secret criteria for redundancy were union members.[49] The IMPACT union has also reported a case where a business student was taken on for three months by the HSE to cover work for a clerical officer on maternity leave. The posting had no relevance to their previous degree.[50] Overall, the JobBridge scheme has experienced a high drop-out rate, with three out of four interns failing to complete their work programme.[51]

Originally social welfare was designed to give people support while they found employment that suited them. However, increasingly new subtle forms of pressure are being designed to compel people to take up posts they do not choose. This can occur through direct sanctions as people are threatened with a reduction in social welfare payments if they do not accept an employment offer. Or there can be an attempt at a wider cultural change so that unpaid work becomes a rite of passage into the labour market. Employers will, naturally, seek to take advantage of such cost-cutting schemes but the consequences of the change go far beyond immediate employer advantage. They are part of a wider mechanism to accustom people to the more brutal realities of twenty-first-century Irish capitalism. Obedience, subservience to authority, lack of choice and above all, lower expectations are the requirements for those who run a failing system.

5

Where Are the Jobs?

'Say "G'Day Mate" this Australia Day for just 15 cents per minute' proclaimed the giant billboard. There was something funny about its location facing the Centra shop at the junction between Galway and Kinvara in 2011. The bleak, rocky Galway landscape did not usually resonate with an elongated twang, but the marketing managers of Meteor knew exactly what they were doing. Emigration has returned to Ireland with over 200 people leaving each day. The country has reverted to its historic role as a labour 'storehouse', this time sending workers not only to Britain but to mining compounds in Australia and the lumber yards of Canada. The money may be good, but the hours are long and the work is tough. Old traditions of emigrant remittances mix with modern Skype calls as another version of the 'American wake' has returned. James Cannon, the owner of the Atlantic Bar in Dungloe, Donegal explains:

We're calling them 'Australian Wakes' here. Nearly every day last week, people left Dungloe for different parts of Australia. Our daughter went just last week to Perth, and the first day she was there she went into a restaurant and ran into someone from Dungloe. She said there's another batch of girls heading out next week.

A lot of lads are trying to get into the mines, where the big money is. They work ten days on, four days off. There's quite a few engineers gone out, and lads in construction and trades. There's more and more talking about going out there. As far as I know, it's mainly single people in their twenties. I haven't heard of any families going out'.[1]

One of the main achievements of the Celtic Tiger was to open up third level education for the majority of the population. Remarkably, Ireland has the highest percentage of people with third level qualifications in the 25 to 34 year age bracket in the EU – 48 per cent compared to an EU average of 33 per cent.[2] While other countries introduced high fees and were saddling young people with loans, the Celtic Tiger kept the cost of entry comparatively low. More working class people were able to send their children on to higher education. The bald figures masked all sorts of inequalities and problems – there is an under-representation of mature students; there is a subtle social divide whereby the children of higher professionals dominate the universities and those of skilled and unskilled manual workers go to the Institutes of Technologies. Nevertheless, the legacy of the Celtic Tiger was a highly educated workforce but the tragedy is that many of these graduates are never going to work in Ireland. Donegal may well be a hot spot of the 'American Wake', but the same ritual is happening across the country as highly qualified candidates head for the emigration planes.

Scandalously, the government does not seem to care. The sole focus of its policy has been bailing the banks out and there has been no serious commitment to a job creation programme. During the Great Depression of the 1930s, it was common sense to believe that the state should intervene to help create employment. In the US, Roosevelt's New Deal put hundreds of thousands to work on building bridges, parks and motorways. In Ireland, de Valera and Fianna Fail proclaimed that it was the duty of the state to guarantee a right to work. These policies found their theoretical justification in the writings of Keynes. This renowned economist had originally adhered to the 'balance the books' orthodoxy and supported cuts in state spending but the Wall Street Crash shook him out of these beliefs. A long economic depression convinced him that the state had to create a 'stimulus programme' to increase consumer demand because only through such a mechanism would the private sector be encouraged to invest. In line with Keynes's idea, many governments introduced public works programmes in the belief that if people were given work, their wages would add to consumption and stimulate further investment.

The Irish government could have followed this path in the present crisis and Michael Taft, an economist with UNITE, explained how.[3]

First off, they could have drawn up an audit for work that needed to be done in childcare, infrastructure development, elder care, and environmental supports. This could then have been started by hiring 50,000 of the long-term employed, offering them a wage just above the legal minimum. Taft calculated that if these people were hired on a weekly 39-hour contract of work and paid €9 per hour, they would receive an annual wage of €18,250. An additional 15 per cent might be added in for administration and this would have meant an initial government outlay of €1.05 billion a year. But this is only a headline figure because the state would save on social welfare spending and there would be a return to the state in taxes and Universal Social Insurance. Increased spending by the newly employed would also help stimulate more economic activity. When these savings were taken into account, Taft estimated that employing 50,000 people on an Employer of Last Resort Scheme would cost between €400 and €500 million. If the government was to double the numbers and take 100,000 off the dole it would come to €1 billion, which is a fraction of the money wasted on zombie banks.

The Irish government, however, chose not to do this. Instead it repeatedly proclaimed as its favourite dogma 'Governments don't create jobs, successful businesses and entrepreneurs do'.[4] It went further and has cut 30,000 public sector jobs and plans to cut another 5000. Instead of replacing jobs lost in the private sector, it adds its own quota to the dole queues. In essence, the government's jobs strategy is based on two words – business confidence. Money poured into banks adds 'confidence' in the financial markets and the more tax breaks given to companies, the greater their 'confidence'. Add in costly public–private partnership programmes and there will be even more 'confidence' at taxpayers' expense. With confidence comes investment and that will bring jobs – or so the theory goes.

There is not the slightest sign that it works. Just fewer than half a million people are currently classified as unemployed, accounting for over 14 per cent of the workforce. This is despite the fact that the labour force has been shrinking annually since the end of the Celtic Tiger. In 2007, there were 2,143,100 people at work, but this has dropped each year to 1,841,000 by the end of 2012.[5] The difference is accounted for, mainly, by the huge numbers of people who have already emigrated since 2008. Yet despite this catastrophe, all official projections drawn up by the government assume that the unemployment rate will remain at somewhere between 13 and 14 per cent of the workforce for some time to come. By the hundredth anniversary of the 1916 rebellion, the legacy of Irish independence will still be mass joblessness. No wonder government officials silently cheer when planeloads of young Irish people fly to Australia or Canada. Emigration, after all, removes the potential malcontents and helps massage the figures downwards.

Government Fraud

The main official response to the jobs crisis has been to harass the unemployed and create an atmosphere where division and scape-goating become rife. This is not done in a crude, direct way because Irish politics is full of people who talk about protecting the 'vulnerable' and the 'socially excluded' but there are other ways to send out signals. One is to present social welfare fraud as a major problem and have the media go on witch-hunting exercises. The Department of Social Protection has launched a major Fraud Initiative 2011–2013 and its Minister, Joan Burton, has ordered her Department to target fraud to the value of at least €625 million'.[6] How she came up with this precise figure was never explained but social welfare inspectors have been calling people in and questioning them at length to meet the artificial target set by their Minister. And, naturally, the targets are not just met but are overfulfilled. The fraud scare is also being used to justify a new identity card project. Bureaucrats have always wanted to keep a close eye on their populations and so the possibility of having everyone carry a biometric card, which contains vast amounts of personal data, thrills them. What better way to start than to force social welfare recipients to have such a Public Services Card on the pretext of preventing fraud.

The reality is that welfare fraud is a manufactured issue – a deliberately induced media creation that has the distinct purpose of fostering social division and the Department's own figures reveal this. The new anti-fraud campaign dramatically increased the case reviews of social welfare recipients, with an extra 365,000 people being reviewed but the amount 'saved' was only an extra €7 million[7]– literally a drop in the ocean in an overall budget of €20 billion. The

Comptroller and Auditor General also assessed social welfare spending and found that €92 million was recorded in overpayments in 2011. That amounts to 0.5 per cent of the total budget, which again is quite small but even this figure is inflated because it includes both overpayment and fraud. *Overpayment* means that genuine mistakes were made either by the social welfare recipient or the social welfare officer whereas *fraud* occurs where claimants deliberately claim money to which they are not entitled. If, as the Comptroller and Auditor General suggests, fraud amounts to 38 per cent of the overpayment cases, then we are down to the startling figures of €35 million or a paltry 0.2 per cent of welfare budget.[8]

Now contrast this with the failure of people to claim what is rightfully theirs. Low paid employees are entitled to supplement their income through the Family Income Supplement (FIS) scheme but a study conducted by the ESRI found that a majority of those eligible did not make a claim.[9] A later study conducted by Millward Brown IMS for the Department of Social Protection suggested the number of people who failed to claim was between 23 per cent and 30 per cent of those eligible. If we use the latter figures and apply them to the estimates for FIS in 2011, then somewhere between €46 million and €60 million is not being claimed.[10] In other words, under-claiming from just one social welfare payment amounts to far more than the money misspent on fraud. The Millward Brown study recommended a public information campaign, consisting of a mailshot to all potential applicants on the Department's database to inform people of their rights.[11] Yet, Joan Burton showed little interest and instead there was a manufactured moral panic over fraud.

The second way to target the unemployed is to talk about the 'over-generous' social welfare payments. Typically a member of the Irish Small & Medium Enterprises (ISME) comes on to radio or television to tell how they could not recruit staff because they are getting too much on social welfare. This is often followed by a series of similar anecdotes to convey an impression that listeners are being taxed heavily to subsidise layabouts and scroungers. Government Ministers never stoop to such low propaganda but they ride that sentiment by taking a more ambiguous position. They don the mantle of 'protecting the vulnerable' by saying they will maintain 'core' social welfare payments but then they follow IMF orders and systematically reduce supplementary benefits such as rental support. However, once again the scapegoating is based on mythology.

The main concept used for measuring the benefit of social welfare is the Net Replacement Rate.[12] This refers to the proportion of a former wage one might receive in social welfare. The OECD produces a database to compare social welfare benefits in its member states. Its primary purpose is to benchmark one against the other – in order to encourage a general reduction. Its own figures, however, show that Ireland is not significantly out of line with countries in the EU 15 – and often is much less generous. A few stylised examples illustrate this from the most recent 2010 figures.

- Social welfare for a single person on a low income is the third worst among the EU 15.[13]
- Social welfare received by one earner on the average wage, who is part of a married couple with no children, lies exactly at the mid-point of the EU 15 scale.
- Social welfare received by one earner on the average, who is part of a married couple with two children, is slightly above the mid-point of the EU 15 scale.
- But the social welfare of two earners on the average wage, who are part of a married couple with two children, is the third worst in the EU 15 – when account is taken of 'top-up' benefits.[14]

Despite these comparisons, the Minister for Social Protection, Joan Burton, has suggested that some of the unemployed have made a 'lifestyle choice'.[15] It is a pity, however, that she never explained why so many decided upon this particular 'choice' in recent years. During the Celtic Tiger, unemployment declined to 4 per cent of the workforce – which is technically equivalent of full employment because it allows for a certain friction in job mobility. So why, suddenly, would so many 'choose' a different lifestyle? The obvious answer is that they did not choose – there are simply not enough jobs. At present, there are 50 people unemployed for every job offer that appears,[16] which gives Ireland one the highest ratios in the EU 15 of unemployed people to job vacancies. Economists define a labour market as 'tight' when employers have to offer incentives to get people to work. Yet in Ireland, it is workers who offer incentives to employers by working for less or, in a small number of cases, even working for €50 a week on top of social welfare on the government's JobBridge programme.

The official unemployment figures disguise an even harsher reality. Many who are seeking full-time employment have settled for part-time employment. Others have become discouraged by the lack of response and have stopped looking. Still others may have a promise of work in the future and cannot take a job today. All of these fit into the category of 'under-employment' and, when added to the officially unemployed, they account for a quarter of the Irish labour force.[17] Ireland comes just behind Spain, Greece and the Baltic states for its waste of willing labour – and it is getting worse. Long-term unemployment – which is defined as being out of work for more than a year – has grown dramatically and now accounts for 60 per cent of those out of work.[18] This has huge implications for social suffering in Ireland.

Social Devastation

There is a vast research literature that documents the adverse effects of unemployment. It shows that unemployment leads to a loss of earnings – but not just in the short term. It suggests that people, who are made unemployed during a recession, will experience an earnings drop of the order of around 20 per cent on average for between 15 and 20 years.[19] This occurs for a variety of reasons. Sometimes skills become obsolete as whole industries get wiped out or heavily reduced. Mature workers who are aged more than 50 may also find it hard to get another job. There is also 'cyclical downgrading' where workers take up worse jobs and get stuck in them. Hardships caused by job loss can also have a serious impact on health. In the short term, unemployment leads to heightened levels of stress and a higher incidence of heart attacks, but data from the US also suggests that an increased mortality rate can persist for up to 20 years afterwards. As a result, a prolonged period of unemployment is closely related to a decline of between 1 and 1.5 years' life expectancy.[20] The key factor is money because, broadly speaking, the poorer you are, the harder it is to maintain a healthy lifestyle but linked to this is the more complex interaction with higher stress levels. Contrary to popular perception, stress is not a condition that is primarily suffered by high flying corporate executives. It tends to disproportionately hit the poor and those in the most subordinated job positions.[21]

In some ways, the greater tragedy is the way in which unemployment affects families and children. Research has found, for example, that there is a negative impact on children's educational performance. One US study found that parental job loss increases the chance of a child repeating a grade by 15 per cent.[22] Another Swedish study found longer-term effects on children's well-being. Surprisingly, the loss of earnings did not just affect the long-term mortality of the parents – but their children as well.[23]

These findings – which are mainly drawn from an economic literature which examines quantitative data – capture some of the most salient external features of unemployment. The classical sociological text on the subject was published by Marie Jahoda *et al.* in 1933. Entitled, *Marienthal: The Sociography of an Unemployed Community,* it told of the social effects of mass unemployment on a factory village in Austria during the Great Depression.[24] The research combined quantitative data with participation by the researchers in the community and an examination of life histories. It particularly focused on the psychic effects of unemployment on well-being. Writing nearly 50 years after *Marienthal* was published, Jahoda summed up the central thesis:

> Employment of whatever kind and at whatever level makes the following categories of psychological experiences inevitable: it imposes a time structure on the waking day; it compels contacts and shared experiences with others outside the nuclear family; it demonstrates that there are goals and purposes which are beyond the scope of an individual, but require a collectivity; it imposes status and social identity through the division of labour in modern employment and, last but not least, it enforces activity.[25]

The absence of work, she argued, removes these vital psychological life supports and disorientates individuals. There may be an element of romanticisation in Jahoda's argument as not *all* work provides the type of support that Jahoda describes but, many of the key salient points remain.

The loss of employment uproots the basic 'time structures' around which individuals pattern their lives. These small daily timetables give meaning, purpose and help to organise our mental life. Once they are removed, resignation and purposeless can take their place. Ironically, although the unemployed have far more spare time on their hands, they often find their time is wasted. There is a sense of drift, a pattern of more aimless pursuits and with it a decline in self-esteem. There is a tendency to withdraw from participation in wider social activity and a decline in 'social capital' – links with individuals outside the immediate family.[26] The effects on the individual from this pattern of social isolation and disorganisation are manifold. Research points to a higher incidence of alcohol disorder,[27] depression, divorce and family conflict.[28]

One of the principal features of the global recession has been youth unemployment. In Ireland, the rate of unemployment among young people is estimated to lie somewhere between 35 per cent and 39 per cent. The latter figure comes from most recent Census findings which also indicated that the figure was at a shocking 49 and 50 per cent in Donegal and Limerick respectively. These figures do not appear in offical unemployment statistics because many young people do not register as unemployed because they receive very low rates of social welfare and are means tested. All of this has huge implications for the future. In the 1960s, protest movements were largely fuelled by white, affluent students whose college degree was meant to offer a chance of a comfortable career. The leitmotif was opposition to the dehumanisation of society, aptly symbolised by US Defence Secretary Robert McNamara's obsession with 'body counts' in the Vietnam war. But there was also a generalised questioning of the wider system, as *The Graduate* exemplified in its portrayal of the alienated boredom of American suburban life. Yet this rebellion was recuperated by a system that sold back a sense of individual freedom and identity to the '68 generation.

Mass youth unemployment in the twenty-first century is producing a different form of rebellion. A chain of protests has appeared that stretches from the Occupy movement in the US to the Indignados movement in Spain to the streets of Cairo and Athens. Mike Davies explains the dynamics:

Some of the occupiers of Zuccotti Park (New York), if they had graduated ten years earlier, might have walked straight into $100,000 salaries at a hedge fund or investment bank. Today they work at Starbucks.

Globally, young adult unemployment is at record levels, according to the ILO – between 25 and 50 per cent in most of the countries with youth-led protests. Moreover, in the North African crucible of the Arab revolution, a college degree is inversely related to likelihood of employment. In other countries as well, family investment in education, when incurred debt is considered, is paying negative dividends.[29]

These dynamics have not yet come into play in Ireland but according to IMF projections, official unemployment will still be at 10 per cent even by 2017.[30] When a society condemns so many of its youth to the boredom and depression of unemployment, can a social revolt be far behind?

6

Will There Be a Roof Over Our Heads?

'Buy your own housing estate at a knock-down price.' This was the message that 20 potential investors heard when they looked at the Glendale estate in Tullow, County Carlow. The whole estate of 63 houses was put up for sale by an unnamed bank and was eventually bought for just over €10,000 a unit. At the peak of the Celtic Tiger, these fine houses might have fetched €200,000 each and so quite a bargain was had.

Every major economic crash creates opportunities for businesses who ride out the storm. They function as scavengers who buy up disused factories, machinery or property at very low prices. These bargain hunters play an important role within the wider system because crashes are often triggered by an over-accumulation of investment in particular sectors. So a clearing out by liquidation of values is the only way to create new opportunities for profit. This is why 'vulture capitalists', who seek out distressed assets, are one of the uglier but necessary sides of modern capitalism.

A number of the vultures have already landed in Ireland and have hired local advisors to assist in the bargain hunting. Apollo Global Management, for example, is a gigantic firm which manages world-wide assets that are equal in value to half the Irish economy and one of its advisors is Brian Goggin, the former chief executive of Bank of Ireland. During the Celtic Tiger, when the bank embarked on a reckless policy of stoking up the property bubble, Goggin was on a salary of €3,998,000 a year. Later, as the crisis engulfed the bank, he walked off into the sunset on an annual pension of €626,000, the equivalent of the wages of 17 average workers. Few will miss the irony of a failed banker advising vulture capitalists on bargain opportunities. His own activities as a bank CEO helped to trigger the crash but, instead of paying for his mistakes, he has been rewarded with new opportunities for money making. Goggin's career transition illustrates, in rather dramatic fashion, the hypocrisy that surrounds the rhetoric about 'moral hazard' emanating from the political establishment. 'Moral hazard' is supposed to mean that there should be no support for those who make poor choices or take risks that go badly wrong yet, strangely, the concept of moral hazard disappeared during the bailout of Ireland's bankers. There was no official demand, for example, to strip the CEOs of Allied Irish Bank and Bank of Ireland of their massive pension pots before taxpayers' money was used to recapitalise them but when it came to any suggestion of state support for people in mortgage distress, there were screams about 'moral hazard'.

Vast numbers of people currently worry that they may not be able to afford the roof over their heads. Through no fault of their own, they may have lost their jobs or experienced a cut in social welfare and can no longer afford huge mortgage payments. Central Bank figures at the end of 2012 showed that 94,488 households are in arrears for more than 90 days and 79,582 had their mortgages 'restructured', which means they have reached an agreement with their lending agency on reduced payments. Nearly half of the latter category had fallen into arrears, despite the fact that the most common form of restructuring was moving to an interest-only payment. In total, there is €111 billion outstanding in Irish mortgages, but if we add together those who are in arrears with those who are restructured, there is a problem in the repayment of €31 billion or 34 per cent of the total.[1] And it is set to get worse for a host of reasons. Over half of Irish mortgages are in negative equity [2] and, despite the regular, cheery reports in the news media, Irish property prices are set to fall further.

One reason is that the Celtic Tiger saw an explosion in landlordism as large swathes of the upper middle class bought property as an investment. They took out big loans in the hope they could sustain or recoup them from rental income. However, as unemployment shot up and property prices crashed, this stratum was left with huge, unsustainable mortgages. Arrears on these buy-to-let properties are running at nearly twice those of homeowners of principal dwellings, with 19 per cent in arrears for more than 90 days.[3] Many landlords have only survived by restructuring to interest-only mortgages but there is a five-year trigger before they must move onto combined interest and principal payments. As this kicks in, many will not be able to pay and so the dumping of large amounts of this landlord property onto the market will lead to further price falls.

In addition, the wider austerity policies have impacted heavily on distressed mortgage payers. Davy Stockbrokers ran a set of figures and found that the strongest correlation was between arrears and long-term unemployment. As the numbers out of work for more than a year grow, so arrears increase exponentially. With 60 per cent of those out of work already categorised as long-term unemployed, Davy's predicts that the numbers in arrears by over 90 days will peak at 16.5 per cent of all mortgages and a staggering 18 per cent in an adverse scenario.[4] Up to now, many have only been able to keep their heads above water because they are on tracker mortgages. This has been beneficial because interest payments have been reduced as the ECB cut rates in the hope of moving the wider European economy out of recession. If there was any significant EU recovery and interest rates rose, half of all Irish mortgage payers would be squeezed further. Homeowners are, therefore, in a classic Catch-22 situation: they wish for an end to the EU-wide recession so there are more jobs; but if the recession ends, interest rates will rise and there will be even bigger mortgage repayments.

All of this suggests a case for government intervention to alleviate this distress. But in neoliberal Ireland, the government insists that there will be no interference in the market – at least for mortgage holders. The predominant discourse has been that there can be no 'blanket debt forgiveness'. Each individual will have to look at their own circumstances, take responsibility for their actions and enter 'meaningful discussions' with their bank or mortgage holder. There will be no write-down of mortgage debt for those who bought at the height of the Celtic Tiger. There is no special fund that is similar to the €75 billion Housing Affordability and Stability Plan in the US designed to give long-term relief. Instead, all the talk is of 'moral hazard' and not allowing one neighbour to piggyback on the taxes of the other. The state's only role apparently lies in providing financial advice and creating a framework whereby individuals come to a resolution with their banks. It has created a panel of over 2700 accountants who will give advice on options but the distressed mortgage holder has to persuade their lender to pay €250 for the service. So instead of action to deal with a vast social problem, a new business opportunity has been created for a vast legal–accountancy axis.

The government has also supported an elite-inspired campaign to step up the rate of evictions. Like a mounting drum-beat, very important people have stepped forward to talk of 'courage' and 'grasping the nettle'. Fiona Muldoon, from the Central Bank called on bankers to 'forget humility' and take 'tough minded' decisions to bring resolution to the arrears issue.[5] John Moran, Secretary General of the Department of Finance, has claimed that there is an 'unnaturally low' level of repossessions in Ireland.[6] Support has also come from the Troika and the IMF, which demanded an 'effective repossession framework' which can take account of the 'positive experience with expedited proceedings for repossessions in the Commercial Court'.[7] The target of this elite campaign was a legal loophole that the group New Beginning found when they took a legal case to protect mortgage holders. Before December 2009, lenders could use a 1964 law to evict people from their homes but this act was repealed and replaced by the Land and Conveyancing Law Reform Act in 2009. However, it subsequently transpired that there was a drafting oversight because it only applied to loans taken out after 1 December 2009. When Justice Elizabeth Dunne heard a case for eviction in July 2011, she noted this loophole and ruled that there could only be repossessions when full repayment had been demanded before December 2009. As a result of this legal quagmire, Ireland has had a far lower rate of evictions than countries like Spain or the US which experienced similar property bubbles. Only 1350 evictions occurred between 2009 and 2012. Too many, certainly – but not enough to satisfy the bankers.

The government's response to this elite campaign is to close the legal loophole and change the mild-mannered Code of Conduct on Mortgage Arrears to make it easier for the banks to take tougher action. A rule that banks can only make three unsolicited calls to the lender per month is being removed. The 12-month moratorium on 'non-co-operating' mortgage payers will also be abolished and banks get greater powers to define who is co-operating and who is not. Banks may also move people off tracker mortgages if they provide customers with alternative longer-terms solutions.[8] New guidelines on reasonable lifestyles have also been issued which explicitly exclude satellite television, giving to charity or sports expenses. The point of these new procedures is to give the banks targets for resolving mortgage distress but on terms which are overwhelmingly favourable to the lenders.

The government has claimed that its new Personal Insolvency Arrangement regime will enable people to write down unsecured debt up to €3 million and exit a bankruptcy after six years. But while this may offer some comfort to the landlords in the buy-to-let sector, it does nothing for homeowners. Banks will retain a veto on any possible write-down and they will get new powers to evict. Slowly but surely Ireland is following a path hewn in the US where removal vans are a regular sight as 5 million homes have been foreclosed.[9] This is all the more tragic because even the conservative government in Spain has had to backtrack on its policy of facilitating evictions after a council worker, Amaia Egana, committed suicide.

The state's justification for embarking on this path draws on two themes that are central to the neoliberal discourse that pervades the political establishment. The first is that the mortgage crisis is a collection of individual problems rather than a collective issue, which the state itself helped to create. The issue of mortgage difficulty is only to be considered on a case by case basis having regard to the individual circumstances of each case. The second assumption is that the market cannot function properly until the artificial situation of people occupying homes they cannot afford is ended. In other words, the hopes and lives of more than 100,000 people who are currently in mortgage distress must be sacrificed to a dogma of free markets. As Davy Stockbrokers put it, 'an increased number of repossessions is desirable to help unlock and add transparency to the illiquid housing market'.[10] By this they mean that proper 'clearing prices' can only be set by the market after thousands of evictions lead to more house sales. Once these 'real' prices are reached, the market will start working again and everything will function smoothly.

Both these propositions are fundamentally flawed. Ireland's housing crisis did not arise from a set of individual choices but from an institutional structure shaped by state policy and bankers' desire for super profits. The nexus that connected the political elite to the builders and bankers was, principally but not exclusively, organised through the Fianna Fail party. It created a framework where people were pushed into buying houses at astronomical prices, precisely because the market made that appear as the most logical option at the time. In government, Fianna Fail introduced a host of tax breaks such as reducing capital gains tax on second homes and Section 23 tax breaks for the write-off of rental income. This stimulated a massive property bubble that coincided with a shift from individual home ownership to landlordism and the use of houses as investment income. At the same time, however, there were severe cutbacks in social housing and a refusal to introduce any form of rental control. In a situation where rents were high and banks were assiduously pushing loans with little scrutiny on people's ability to pay, tens of thousands fell for the line about 'getting their foot on the property ladder'.

Those who focus on individual responsibility sometimes claim that the Irish have an irrational fixation with property. The history of British landlordism, it is suggested, has left such a powerful scar that almost every Irish person aspires to own their own home. Home ownership, it is claimed, is just part of the Irish psyche. This cultural reflex, apparently 'got out of hand' during the Celtic Tiger years and the combination of a post-colonial legacy and 'individual choice' caused the problem. This story-line, however, is a myth. Far from the Irish having an innate desire for home ownership, thousands of people have lived in social housing in recent history. Between 1932 and 1942, for example, local authorities provided 60 per cent of the housing output and up to the mid 1950s public provision of housing exceeded 50 per cent of new homes. The creation of a conservative, home owning democracy did not arise from an automatic cultural reflex but was part of a deliberate state strategy which sought to encourage private house ownership. This eventually melded into an orgy of property speculation during the latter phases of the Celtic Tiger. State policy was entirely directed to stimulating the private housing sector and by 2006 public provision had declined to just 6 per cent of all housing units. The extraordinary property bubble that nearly swallowed the Irish economy cannot, therefore be explained by individual choice. Between January 1996 and December 2005, 553,267 housing units were built in Ireland. And then, despite the fact that a quarter of a million units were unoccupied, another 244,590 units were added between January 2006 and December 2009.[11] At the height of the bubble, Ireland was building twice as many units per head of population as elsewhere in Europe. This phenomenon could only have been a direct result of a state policy that pressurised people to buy homes at absurd prices.

Nor did market mechanisms – which, it is now claimed, can solve the problem – rectify it. According to conventional economics, an oversupply of any good or service should lead to a fall in price as the market corrects itself. But the opposite occurred during the Celtic Tiger. New house prices rose in Dublin by 429 per cent while the price of second-hand houses in the same city rose by 551 per cent between 1991 and 2007.[12] The increases could not be explained by rises in the cost of building material or labour as these had only doubled in the same period. Land prices were a factor as Irish land became the most expensive in Europe but the inflation in land prices was not the result of a restriction in supply, as market fundamentalists might argue. There was often a largely unrestricted planning system which allowed builders to construct houses in the most inappropriate locations. At the core of the problem was the near monopoly control of land by a small number of builders on the outskirts of major cities. The tight grip which developers, bankers and politicians held over the wider economy drove the property bubble forward in a mad rush for super profits.

The result of this madness is not only mortgage distress but long-term chaos that affects health and the environment. The property bubble forced many to live in the commuter belts of Dublin and the other cities. They moved to areas which had few facilities and poor infrastructure on, what they hoped, would be a temporary basis, but the effect of this 'suburbanisation' was that the private car became a necessity for survival. People drive for hours to work; they drive to large shopping malls on the outskirts of towns; they drive to meet friends and family. Ireland has become one of the most private car-dependent societies in the world with 73 per cent of all journeys made by car, and only 4 per cent by bus and 1 per cent by rail and bicycle.[13] It has created an 'obesogenic' environment and Ireland's adult obesity rate is now higher than 18 states of America. One of the main reasons is that there is less time for spontaneous exercise because so much time is spent commuting.

Those who seek a return to the primacy of the market have also forgotten the victims of the Celtic Tiger's lax planning regime. Some of these live in houses built on flood plains because councils rezoned land to create 'fields of gold' for developers. Others live in houses which contain pyrite, a material which expands causing structural damage. Despite the fact that concerns had been long expressed in Britain and Canada, Irish building regulations did not outlaw pyrite and up to 60,000 properties are affected.[14] Still others live in areas where there are no adequate wastewater treatment facilities because nearly half of Ireland's facilities are below national and EU standards.[15] Still others find themselves in the 1655 ghost estates or, as the Department of Environment defines them, 'unfinished developments with substantial construction work outstanding'.[16]

This massive social wreckage of mortgage distress, involuntary suburbanisation, and poor quality building cries out for a break from the neoliberal mindset. Instead of repeating hypocritical platitudes about 'moral hazard' and setting up a framework to increase evictions, the government should intervene to help those in mortgage distress. If €64 billion can be made available to bail out banks, there can be no argument against banks now scaling down mortgages to the values that pertained in 2003 or 2004. There is nothing to stop a government drawing up transparent criteria by which people would apply for such relief and, therefore, no need for a 'case by case' approach. Such relief should be confined to owners of a principal dwelling, not buy-to-let properties. More generally, a major public works programme is required to rectify the damage done by the state's abnegation of its planning responsibilities during the Celtic Tiger era. More public transport infrastructure is needed to deal with suburbanisation; remedial work needs to be done on ghost estates; proper public investment is required for wastewater facilities. And all of this could have been done for a fraction of the money spent on bailing out banks.

It could still be done if the state repudiated the debt imposed on it by the EU elite. Yet under the current status quo this will never happen. Instead, they will look on silently as vulture capitalists descend on the country to buy up housing estates and distressed assets. And they will cry moral hazard when asked to help the little people.

7

Tax Haven Capitalism

Global capitalism has entered a new era where there are more frequent economic crises. The failure of whole swathes of the system to make a rapid recovery from the crash of 2008 indicates that it faces deeper long-term problems. Irish capitalism, however, is particularly weak and in this chapter we shall examine how it is increasingly reliant on functioning as a tax haven for corporations and wealthy individuals. This will take us on a somewhat technical journey through the complexities of tax evasion. It will also involve some jumps from the Irish economy to the US and back again. Our overall argument is that Ireland's clean image is only sustained through a nod and wink culture at the very top – and that this is no basis on which to build a sustainable economy matching the aspirations of its people.

'The customer is king' is a motto that businesspeople regularly repeat. It echoes the claim that capitalism is built on 'choice' and merely supports consumer needs. In reality, the system is driven by an endless, restless search for profit. The drive to expand capital is the primary goal and the satisfaction of human needs is only a by-product. To illustrate, let us consider the pattern of lending to non-financial corporations in Ireland during the Celtic Tiger years between 1999 and 2007. Credit is the lifeblood of the economy as it facilitates its expansion. The more credit that is available, the quicker the circuit of production and realisation of profit can be completed and renewed again. So the allocation of credit between different sectors can tell us a lot about where capitalists think they should invest.

Table 7.1 covers the most successful epoch for Irish capitalism and so all sectors show growth. There is an astounding contrast, however, between the supply of credit to manufacturing and the supply to

Table 7.1: Selected Sectoral Breakdown of Non-Financial Corporation
Loans 1999 and 2007. Stock of loans (€million) and
Percentage Change

	1999	2007	% Change
Manufacturing	4,498	8,095	80
Construction	1,962	24,351	1141
Wholesale/Retail Trade and Repairs	3,331	12,103	263
Hotels and Restaurants	2,677	10,537	293
Real Estate	3,594	71,833	1899

Source: R. McElligott and R. Stuart, 'Measuring the sectoral distribution of lending to Irish
non-financial corporates', Central Bank Financial Stability Report 2007, pp. 115–26.

construction and real estate. Credit to manufacturing grew by 80 per
cent during the period and covered the cost of depreciation of machinery, the creation of new factories and purchase of new equipment. But
it is dwarfed by a 1899 per cent increase to real estate and a 1,141 per
cent increase to construction. In 1999, a third of all lending to Irish
capitalists went to these two categories but, by 2007, this had jumped to
three-quarters. Even this bald figure underestimates the scale of the
amazing shift because much of the credit for hotels and restaurants, for
example, was used for speculative building purposes. If we use a
different calculation and look at the net capital stock in different
sectors, we again find that in 2007, 65 per cent is concentrated in construction and real estate as against only 6 per cent in manufacturing.[1]

Capital and credit ultimately accrue from the energy, toil and work
of hundreds of thousands of people who create and transform nature
with their hands and brains. We might reasonably ask why the fruits of
their collective labour were overwhelmingly diverted into property –
leading to an inevitable crash. A rather feeble attempt was made to
provide an explanation based on the concept of consumer demand. In
March 2006, NCB stockbrokers claimed that there was 'no evidence of
speculative building' and that the surge in house building was driven
by demography.[2] A growth in the population aged over 25 and mass
immigration, they claimed, created the demand that Irish builders set
out to satisfy. The crash, which occurred a year after the report was
issued, came as a total surprise because, presumably, there was still the

same number of young people and migrants as before. The real explanation, of course, did not lie in 'consumer demand' because construction was not driven by human need but rather a frenzy of speculation. The diversion of investment into property was driven by the lure of huge profits and was heavily subsidised by the state.

Construction and property offer a number of attractions for Irish capitalists. First, the building industry is a better protected sector than others as it is more difficult to import cement and bulky materials than, say, washing machines or computers. Irish capitalists who invested in construction were, therefore, sheltered from the full rigors of competition on the global markets. Second, the property market is more easily influenced by state intervention. The capital-spending programmes of the state or its taxation policy can quickly expand the market. The state is also a major landlord and where it decides to rent can have a major impact on individual property values. At a local level, decisions on land rezoning can bring about major financial gains. Political relations are, therefore, a necessary part of business in this sector and the Irish wealthy are more than adept at establishing these connections.

Third, property speculation creates the possibility of short-term profits. Large loans can be taken from banks and repaid quickly if the market is booming. Simon Kelly, son of the property developer Paddy Kelly, summed up the mentality, 'When the market heated up, buying meant winning: every time you bought land, you made money. It seemed as easy as that'.[3] Irish capitalists, therefore, saw property as nearly risk free, with little capital tied up in machinery over an extended period. To engage in property speculation you needed a friendly banker and Anglo Irish Bank, which was described as the 'lender of choice' for the new entrepreneurial class, played the lead role.[4] Even before the property boom had started, Anglo had backed businesspeople such as Denis O'Brien and Dermot Desmond and was intimately connected to the 'new rich'. Its strategy was 'relationship banking' which meant it developed close social ties with a small number of very wealthy developers. The bank expanded these personalised networks so that eventually nearly all the 'top people' of the country were to be seen at its annual golf outing in Druids Glen.[5]

As Anglo forged ahead, the older banks cast off their staid image and joined the fray. Between 2003 and 2006, Anglo Irish increased its loan book at an annual compound rate of 45 per cent, but Allied Irish Bank oversaw a 34 per cent increase and Bank of Ireland was only slightly more cautious with 27 per cent.[6] The loans were mainly for property, for commercial property in particular, and crucially, to a limited number of key developers. This was, in fact, the distinctive feature of the Irish crash. The small size of the country, the culture of face-to-face networking and the personalised nature of Irish business meant that only a tiny number of people were involved but they had colossal ambitions and an insatiable desire for profit. In the mid 1990s, for example, Irish property speculators had invested less than €100 million in the European property markets. By 2006, however, they had €5.5 billion in British commercial property alone.[7]

This orgy of property speculation was the culmination of many trends that lay at the heart of Irish capitalism. Historically, it is heavily reliant on state support. It seeks short-term profits. It has a grossly over-inflated financial sector. It moves money out of Ireland and has little interest in the broad-based development of the country. And its real productive base is very weak – and getting weaker. The crash was the culmination of many longer-term trends within Irish capitalism.

A Weak Capitalism

Modern Ireland has an extremely weak industrial base. Total employment in the labour force has grown from 1,220,000 in 1926 to 2,143,000 at the high point of the Celtic Tiger before shrinking again to 1,841,000 in 2011. But within that broad pattern, employment in manufacturing industry has been declining both absolutely and relatively.

Approximately the same number are employed in manufacturing today as were employed in 1958, when the Irish state admitted that its protectionist strategy had failed and turned to foreign investment as its principal mechanism for economic development. The numbers employed have also dropped considerably compared to 1981, which, coincidentally, was the year when the Telisis report was published. This had warned against an over-reliance on foreign investment and called

Table 7.2: Employment in Manufacturing, 1951–2011

Year	Number of Workers
2011	181,486
2002	244,203
1991	218,725
1981	238,144
1971	198,377
1961	179,436
1951	184,194

Source: CSO, Census of Population, *Various Years.*

for a shift to an indigenous manufacturing base that could export.[8] Yet Irish capitalism singularly failed to make this turn despite efforts by the state to pick 'national champions' that would break into global markets. There was a temporary growth in the numbers employed in manufacturing when there was a big influx of US investment in the late 1990s and a highpoint was reached in 2002, but thereafter there has been a calamitous decline. Even before the crash, the numbers employed in manufacturing had begun to drop significantly. In fact, the absolute figures disguise the sheer scale of that failure. Today just 8.25 per cent of the Irish workforce is involved in manufacturing.

Manufacturing is divided into 'modern' and 'traditional' sectors, and these are code words for foreign multinational and Irish owned. When this breakdown is examined, the abject failure of Irish capitalists is even starker. Their activities are concentrated in a number of very small areas such as food processing, paper and textiles/clothing. If food processing is excluded, Irish capitalist investment in manufacturing accounts for just 3 per cent of the value added to the Irish economy in 2007.[9] The reliance on the food sector is advantageous when food prices are rising due to speculation and the creation of new markets in India and China. But it also conforms to a very traditional role imposed on Ireland and indicates a failure to diversify.

The multinational sector is geared to the export market but is heavily concentrated on a small number of areas – principally, chemicals, pharmaceuticals and medical devices. Between them they account for 84 per cent of Irish exports and are the engine behind Ireland's export success story. There are major problems ahead, however, because the key sector is pharmaceuticals and it is based on the sale of branded drugs. Crucially, as we have seen, a number of the major products are coming out of their patent lifespan and this will have a major impact on sales. When the patent for the cholesterol-fighting drug Lipitor ended, for example, Ireland's export figures declined by 9 per cent.[10] More broadly, five of the world's top selling drugs which are produced in Ireland are due to come out of patent shortly and sales figures are set to decline by $26 billion in 2013.[11]

Ireland's manufacturing base is, therefore, extremely small and fragile. It is dependent on a score of multinational firms and it is by no means clear that their production figures for Ireland are as large as they appear. Some might argue that this weakness is not a problem as it has become fashionable to denigrate the role of manufacturing with claims that we have moved to a 'post-Fordist' economy or information society. However, manufacturing typically involves a horizontal expansion as it necessitates the supply of components and, sometimes, stimulates the creation of further downstream industries. The increased productivity of manufacturing – which comes from greater capital investment – creates the space for an expansion of services. If developing countries such as Korea or China had foresworn an involvement in manufacturing, it is doubtful if they would be hailed as success stories today.

A Service Economy

Capitalism in Ireland is principally based on services and this is sometimes held up as a sign of maturity. The assumption is that the dirty, smoke-stacked factories have given way to a cleaner, more post-industrial economy. Peripheral countries that missed out on the Industrial Revolution, supposedly, find themselves at an advantage as they leap-frog over the archaic age of factories. For some, the shift to a services economy renders all discussion by Adam Smith or Karl Marx on labour and value as entirely obsolete. For others, such as Daniel Bell, it becomes the springboard to a capitalist utopia because the face-to-face nature of the services leads to a more altruistic ethos.[12] Services, however, are a very broad category that can range from sweeping streets to designing high fashion. The category tells us little about the social relations that exist between workers and employers or even the type of profit making that exists. A more detailed inquiry is necessary.

Here a number of difficulties present themselves because Irish economic statistics are sometimes opaque, for both deliberate and accidental reasons. Take, for example, the issue of holding companies that control dividends and royalties from subsidiary companies that may be located in different parts of the world. Major corporations such as Accenture or Ingersoll Rand have established holding companies in Ireland yet the Central Statistics Office does not provide information about this general category in recent years. In the past they did so and, at the latest date, 2004, there were 2,128 people working for holding companies but thereafter the information is withheld for 'confidential reasons' and no explanation is provided for why a set of figures that was once in the public domain has been removed. More broadly, little information is provided on profit levels or the amount of capital invested in specific subsectors. A technique of agglomeration – where there is no breakdown of big, very general categories – is also used to hide data. The data for these larger, agglomerated categories are mainly based on surveys of business rather than a strict requirement to present accurate information from accounts. Companies are legally obliged to answer surveys – but no sanctions are invoked if they tell blatant untruths to the statistical authorities. Our knowledge on the detailed structure of the economy is, therefore, somewhat limited. Nevertheless we can acquire some picture on how Irish capitalism functions primarily as a services economy.

Services account for, roughly, three-quarters of the gross value added to the Irish economy while industry accounts for one quarter. The term 'services' sometimes conveys an image of high tech modernity with educated graduates but the vast bulk of capital deployed in Irish services is in the traditional areas of wholesale, retail, the motor trade, hotels and catering. The gross value added of these sectors in 2007 amounted to €22.1 billion and they employed 460,234 workers, with Irish capital playing the stronger role. It was concentrated in a number of large companies such as Musgraves or Dunnes in wholesale and retail or the Doyle group in hotels. Irish capital also monopolised the franchises for the motor industry because winning a car dealership from a major conglomerate was often the surest way to making profit. It was a matter of setting up on the edge of a modest sized town and charging over the odds prices for cars. In the hotel industry, Irish capital was lured by the promise of seven-year tax write-offs to produce an incredible oversupply of bed space. Between 1999 and 2002, an extra 26,802 new rooms were added to the hotel register, with an estimated total investment of €5.2 billion and debt of €4.1 billion.[13]

The dominance of these sectors exposes the mythology about an Irish information society. Far from developing high tech, 'immaterial' services, Irish capitalists stick to relatively protected zones where competition is more difficult to organise. In the past, they faced little foreign investment in retail, motors, and hotels. The prolonged boom, however, attracted more foreign investment and Irish capital is now facing a rearguard action to defend itself from the British and German-based retail giants like Tesco, Aldi or Lidl. Their response has been to try to cut wages and drive down working conditions. These sectors were already relatively low paid before the crash, with the hotel and catering industry paying just above the average industrial wage. But after the crash, employers sought to reduce the earnings of workers further by effectively eliminating Sunday payments and gaining greater flexibility on overtime payments.

The discourse about the modernity of the Irish services sector and the creation of an information society is really based on two subsectors which are grouped together as Computing and Related Activities and Other Business Activities. These two categories accounted for 60 per cent of services exports in 2007 and were thought to be at the cutting edge of a high tech economy. Ireland apparently was 'Inching closer to becoming Europe's offshore Silicon Valley' and even a cool-headed academic such as Sean O'Riain, professor of Sociology at the National University of Ireland, Maynooth (NUIM), argued that the 'Irish software industry represents a very significant departure from previous eras in Irish industrial development' as its growth figures appeared to resemble India and Israel.[14]

However, while the Irish software industry showed some expansion during the Celtic Tiger boom, its growth was more solid than dramatic. By 2007, gross value added amounted to €2.2 billion and 18,764 workers were employed – which was nearly the same as the number employed as industrial cleaners. Yet while there were celebratory headlines about the new 'silicon valley', there were few about the old world of cleaners. Moreover, a subtle division emerged within the sector. Smaller Irish start-up companies were often bought up by larger multinationals and their innovative products were relocated to the US or elsewhere. Increasingly, the software industry came to be dominated by bigger firms that hired Irish workers to engage in the localisation of programmes developed elsewhere. By 2007, for example, 94 per cent of the gross value added in this sector was coming from foreign firms that employed 16,153 of the workers while Irish companies were employing fewer than 2,600. Noting these changes, O'Riain later argued that 'Judged by its own criteria of employment creation and industry development, Irish innovation policy in the 2000s had only seen very limited success in the face of admittedly difficult conditions'.[15]

The other area associated with an 'immaterial' information society is known as Other Business Activities and is more intriguing. At the high point of the Celtic Tiger in 2007, it included key groups such as architects, engineers and technical consultancy – which accounted for 24,895 jobs – alongside other auxiliary business functions such as advertising, recruitment agencies and call centres. However, at the core of this sector is a legal, accountancy and tax consultancy nexus and the figures are truly extraordinary. A staggering 84,820 people are employed in this area – or, to put it more starkly, more than a third of the manufacturing workforce. Their combined labour accounted for €8 billion in gross added value to the Irish economy – or 5 per cent of the total.

This is a highly unusual figure but it takes us deep into the heart of Irish capitalism. Ireland's key niche role within global capitalism is to facilitate corporations reducing their taxes on profits. That way they do not pay so much to support schools, hospitals and social welfare in their own country. There is a vast army of tax planners and legal experts who search for 'loopholes' to lessen the tax payments of their clients. This huge, unproductive stratum is intimately connected to the higher echelons of the state and is involved in detailed conversations on how Ireland can offer greater tax subsidies to corporations than other countries. A minor but highly symbolic example illustrates how the system works.

In the budget of 2011, the state agreed to provide tax relief to foreign executives who sent their children to private schools. Fees of up to €5,000 a year could be written off and, in addition, 30 per cent of all income accruing to foreign executives up to €500,000 a year was automatically written off for tax purposes, representing a potential saving of €52,275. All of this was introduced against a background of extreme austerity as single parents, those on rental income supplement, and social welfare recipients experienced significant falls in their income in the same budget. On the surface, this was a strange decision but the internal manoeuvring that preceded it was even more extraordinary. Moves to bring about the change were led by two accountancy firms, Deloitte and KPMG and were backed up by the American Chamber of Commerce and Citibank. In March 2011, John Bradley, a tax partner at KPMG sent a letter to Gary Tobin, head of the business tax team at the Department of Finance, with detailed amendments to existing tax laws which eventually underpinned alternative legislation. On receipt, the Department of Finance immediately drew up calculations based on figures supplied by KPMG. Then, in April, KPMG informed the state officials of a special tax relief scheme they had negotiated with the government of the Netherlands and sent on a copy to the Irish Department with a note which stated, 'This is a good example of the competition which Ireland Inc. faces in this space.'[16] It suggested that the Irish system 'looks very clumsy compared to the Dutch offering'.[17] By December, the desired changes were incorporated in the budget but instead of expressing the slightest gratitude, KPMG complained about the cap on the tax relief set at €500,000 a year. 'Do we want the important people to come here but not the really, really important people' they plaintively moaned.[18]

The comparative ease by which the operation was pulled off illustrates an important aspect of Irish capitalism: granting tax relief to corporations is seen as natural and normal. There was little outcry in Dail Eireann about an accountancy firm drafting legislation for a sovereign government. The population were told that this is just how the world works. This normalisation of the unusual arises from a deep ideology that sees state subservience to multinationals as the key to economic development. The huge tax planning nexus provides the support base to articulate and disseminate this ideology throughout society. What is sometimes referred to as the 'Dublin 4' outlook draws heavily on this social base and expresses itself through a liberal cosmopolitanism that is supposed to define the modern sector of Ireland. This layer in turn intermeshes with the elite of the public sector who share a similar outlook. From the Industrial Development Authority (IDA), to the Department of Finance, to the Clearing House Group in the Department of the Taoiseach to the business section of the Revenue Commissioners there is a strong understanding that Ireland will do what it takes to help corporations dodge taxes. Presented in these bald and stark terms, it sounds somewhat crass but, of course, ideological understandings never quite work like this. They are masked and reconfigured with broader concepts that draw on appeals to patriotism and economic rationality. Thus, the claim that Ireland Inc. is facilitating the robbery of the poor in other countries is diffused by an argument that Ireland's national interest must come first. And whereas that national interest was once defined in terms of the unification of Ireland or the restoration of the national language, today the key terms are economic. Ireland must do what it takes to be 'competitive' within the global economy and only through so doing will it be able to provide jobs for its people. To see why this ideology masks, rather than illuminates, reality, we need to examine Ireland's role in the global tax-dodging network in more detail.

Corporate Tax Dodging

After World War II ended in 1945, there was an acceptance among elites that corporate profits should be taxed to fund the creation of a welfare state or at least provide some social supports for the mass of the population. There was a fear that if concessions were not made, radical movements would emerge. As the British conservative politician, Quintin Hogg, put it, 'If you do not give the people social reform, they will give you revolution.'[19] Moreover, the system was entering its golden age, a major period of expansion which allowed it to grant reforms. So, even in the US, corporate income taxes accounted for nearly a quarter of all federal government receipts.[20] However, with the globalisation of capitalism, this implicit accord was torn up. Corporate tax receipts in the US have declined to just 7 per cent of federal tax revenue with individuals paying six times as much in revenue as the large corporations. Goldman Sachs is a more extreme but, not entirely untypical, example.[21] In 2008, it reported profits of over $2 billion yet paid just over just 1 per cent of this in tax, whilst rewarding its chief executive, Lloyd Blankfein, a staggering $45 million in salaries and bonus. As if this was not bad enough, Goldman Sachs had received a $10 billion handout from US taxpayers, but it still drove its taxes down. The key technique in reducing tax is to move business activity out of high tax jurisdictions, like the US, to countries which have lower tax regimes – or, as Goldman Sachs put it, to create 'changes in its geographical earnings mix'.[22] A study commissioned by the US Senate indicated that the effective tax rate for foreign-sourced income for large corporations was just 4 per cent.[23] The reason is that much of their income is routed through an estimated 60 tax havens which can be defined as sovereign states or (protectorates) which deliberately write laws to attract financial transactions from non-residents. Typically, they provide easy mechanisms for legal incorporation; low or zero tax rates for non-residents; and a shroud of secrecy. Although they are sometimes referred to as 'offshore', they do not always lie geographically apart from the main centres of capital accumulation. Switzerland, after all, lies at the centre of Europe and so 'offshore' effectively means subject to low regulation.

The origins of tax havens go back to the nineteenth century when the US states of Delaware and New Jersey introduced special laws for the easy incorporation of companies. In the 1920s, the impoverished Swiss canton of Zug spread the practice to Europe and it remains to this day one of the major centres where companies claim to be based. However the main impetus came with the decline of the British Empire. While the sun was setting on its imperial grandeur, legislative loopholes were created to allow companies registered with the City of London to escape tax. This enabled the City to preserve its role as a kingdom of finance even as the geographical empire declined. This role expanded greatly after the creation of a Euro-dollar market in the 1960s when US corporations decided to leave money in the City rather than repatriate it to the US where they faced a 15 per cent tax on interest earned abroad. This helped to create a vast pool of finance that was unregulated, available for speculation and above all, untaxed.

Nicholas Shaxson has developed a typology to describe the network of tax havens that currently operate.[24] There is, first, a dense web that radiates out from the City of London with two inner rings and an outer ring. In the former belong the Crown dependencies of Jersey, Guernsey and the Isle of Man and the Overseas Territories of the Cayman Islands, British Virgin Islands, and Bermuda. On the outer ring belong independent states that have a historic connection with Britain. These include Hong Kong, Singapore, the Bahamas, Dubai and, crucially, Ireland. Second, there is the European hub of tax havens that is centred on Luxembourg, Liechtenstein and Switzerland. The Netherlands also plays a crucial role as a conduit for passing funds from one tax haven to another or recycling funds back to high tax countries after they have been cleansed of taxable money. Third, there is another web of tax havens centred on the US sphere of influence. These include local states such as Delaware and Nevada and outer havens such as Panama. Finally, there is a miscellaneous group in Africa and Latin America.

Over half of all banking assets and a third of all Foreign Direct Investment in the world passes through tax havens.[25] And an incredible $21 trillion of the world's wealth is salted away in these havens – the equivalent of one and a half times the US economy.[26] Officially, tax avoidance is frowned upon because everyone is supposed to abide by a patriotic duty to contribute to the upkeep of his or her society. Yet tax dodging on this scale could only take place because state authorities connive with corporations. It works through an official double-speak, whereby a distinction is made between tax *avoidance*, which is seen as a perfectly legal game, and tax *evasion* which is deemed to be illegal. The distinction, however, is artificial because some states construct their laws to allow for tax dodging and so render a wide range of activities perfectly legal.

Efforts by the Organisation for Economic Co-operation and Development (OECD) to stamp out the problem of 'tax havens' shows just how feeble the official opposition really is. In 1998, it issued a report on *Harmful Tax Competition: An Emerging Global Issue* and established a forum.[27] However, the wealthy mounted a lobbying campaign in the US and the Bush regime withdrew from the OECD initiative. The OECD then moved from a 'confrontational' approach to one of treating the tax havens as 'partners'. It urged countries to sign

Tax Information Exchange Agreements with each other and took this as a sign of legitimacy. These agreements are based on written requests for specific information over a particular time period. There was no automatic exchange of information and it was a deliberately cumbersome process. The OECD then developed a blacklist of countries that failed to comply and after a G20 summit in 2009, which threatened economic sanctions, the tax havens collectively signed up to more than 300 agreements. The blacklist was subsequently revised and not even the Cayman Islands, a much cited tax haven, were subject to sanction.

Ironically, the OECD's campaign against tax havens and their subsequent retreat proved beneficial for Ireland. While the value of deposits in global tax havens remained constant, the 'crackdown' led to a shift in funds to countries that had more tax 'legitimate' treaties.[28] Ireland has a high number of older, more useful treaties compared to other countries and so has seen an influx of funds. It has, for example, a tax treaty with the US – whereas the Cayman Islands do not.[29] This arises from the particular niche the country has within the global tax-dodging system. Essentially, Ireland masquerades as an open, transparent and clean country that does not fit into the same category as disreputable places such as Bermuda or the British Virgin Islands. It officially rejects the label of 'tax haven' and offers its clients the aura of European regulation and respectability – while providing enough loopholes to help dodge taxes.

This ambiguity is best illustrated in the manner in which it is sometimes included and sometimes excluded in lists of tax havens. On 4 May 2009, for example, the White House issued a press statement promising a major crackdown on tax havens. It stated that 'nearly one third of all foreign profits reported by US corporations come from just three small, low tax countries: Bermuda, Netherlands and Ireland'.[30] But the next day this sentence was removed after lobbying by the Dutch – and possibly, the Irish embassies. Three years later, however, Obama's re-election team listed Ireland as a tax haven when they highlighted Mitt Romney's $26 billion investment in the Goldman Sachs Liquid Reserves Fund in Dublin.[31] Yet after lobbying by the Irish embassy in Washington, the designation 'tax haven' was again changed to a 'low tax country'.[32] A briefing document produced by the Department of Finance's Tax Strategy Group has also traded on the same ambiguity when it boasted that 'we are not regarded as a tax haven by the United States or any of the other major industrialised countries of the world. This is evidenced by the large and growing number of tax treaties that Ireland has in place with other countries.'[33]

However, the number of tax treaties a country signs tells us very little because the purpose of many of these treaties is to facilitate tax dodging. Ireland has become a specialist in facilitating tax avoidance and this niche role has, tragically, become the centrepiece of its development strategy. In the past, low taxes on corporation profits were seen as a quick way of attracting foreign investment and building up an industrial base, but now, production and services is increasingly organised as an adjunct to tax dodging. Through the creation of a relatively small number of jobs, multinationals can add 'economic substance' to their tax dodge schemes and evade US sanctions. The complexity and deviousness of this strategy has been hidden from the majority of the Irish population because it is located at a micro level that few care to examine.

How Ireland's Tax Haven Works

The most visible sign of Ireland's tax status is the 12.5 per cent rate on corporation profits. Originally, a low rate of 10 per cent was confined to manufacturing exports but in 1997, Charlie McCreevy, the Minister for Finance, established a 12.5 per cent rate for all traded income. The immediate beneficiaries were the banks, who saw a dramatic fall in taxes on their profits, but soon the low corporate tax rate became the great sacred cow of Irish politics. It was supposed to be the key to job creation and no 'bureaucrat in Brussels' was to be allowed to undermine it.

Ireland has the lowest rate of corporation profits tax in the OECD and it is rivalled in Europe only by countries like Cyprus and Bulgaria. The main impact of this tax rate has been to act as a headline invitation to multinationals. It is not, however, the sole reason why they locate in Ireland, because other countries have also dropped their rate of corporation tax. Ironically, Ireland's low tax rate contributed to this global pattern of tax dumping. Between 1995 and 2005, corporate tax rates have dropped on average about 1 per cent a year as companies played one country off against another. Ireland's 12.5 per cent rate is no longer spectacularly lower than Poland, Hungary, the Czech Republic or Slovakia where the rate is 19 per cent and where wage rates are much lower.[34]

Despite the oft-repeated mantra about the 12.5 per cent rate, the reality is quite different. Table 7.3 illustrates how the effective rate is far lower.

In 2008, €66 billion was declared in profits but just less than €4 billion was paid in tax. That amounts to an effective tax rate of 6 per cent – which is half the official rate. Table 7.3 also gives some indication for how this reduction is achieved. The four main categories used to reduce tax on profit are allowances, losses, deductions and reliefs. When a company suffers losses – as many did with the crash – they can be stored up and used to claim tax relief. Losses in one part of a company can also be used to reduce taxes in other subsidiary entities. Only a small proportion of the losses that can be written off for tax purposes were used in 2008 and so far more can be used in the future. There is also a host of other deductions and reliefs and this is where Ireland's vast army of 'tax planners' come into play. Ireland's many tax attractions are made available to both the multinationals and Irish business by planners who charge substantial fees but it would be a mistake to think that they simply wait to see how the state acts and then interpret laws to best suit their clients. Irish tax laws are consciously written to provide relief for corporations both from Ireland's own laws

Table 7.3: Corporation Tax for Accounting Period Ending 2008 (€million)

Profits	66,188
Minus various allowances used in current year	8,978
Total Income and Gains	57,210
Deductions of Taxable Income	5,241
Gross Tax Due	5,076
Reliefs	1,058
Tax Payable	4,004
Tax Received	3,923

Source: Revenue Commissioners, Statistical Report 2010, Corporation Tax Distribution Statistics, p. 5.

– through the creation of 'loopholes' – and from the tax laws of other countries. This is evident in the manner in which the Revenue Commissioners actively collude with the tax planners.

Those charged with gathering taxes on behalf of the state meet five times a year with the poachers who act for corporations via the Consultative Committee of Accountancy Bodies-Ireland and the Irish Tax Instititute. They meet in an official committee known as the Tax Administration Liaison Committee (TALC) and engage in a dialogue that facilitates the planners' clients. The Revenue Commissioners not only helpfully clarify the details of tax legislation to those who are paid to avoid tax but it also takes on board their concerns. In September 2012, for example, tax planners expressed displeasure at the 'treatment of income arising from having or exercising the public office of director of an Irish incorporated company'.[35] Apparently some directors received imbursement through services companies and were somewhat miffed about being personally taxed. If the state believed its own rhetoric about 'sharing the burden', the tax planners would have been given a stern lecture about patriotic duty and shown the door. But this is Ireland and the Revenue Commissioners merely asked for examples so they could 'review the matter in detail'. They then gave a broad hint they would look at the issue of retrospection.[36]

The main country that Ireland tailors its tax legislation for is the US. Despite its role as a bastion of neoliberalism, the US has one of the highest rates of corporation taxes in the world, second only to Japan. Moreover, it uses 'Controlled Foreign Corporation' legislation to tax income sent to parent companies from foreign subsidiaries. This means that, officially, the US taxes its citizens and corporations on a global basis. However, like much else in tax laws all is not what it appears because the US also allows companies to indefinitely 'defer' the income from these subsidiaries. In practice, as one expert put it 'US tax on foreign earnings can be deferred indefinitely and without regard to natural lifespan'.[37] This leads to the phenomenon of 'lock-out' whereby corporations build up huge cash reserves outside the US and use these to engage in acquisitions of other corporations or financial speculation. One study by J. P. Morgan accounting analysts found that at least 60 per cent of the cash balances of large US companies are held overseas.[38] But even as corporations draw on cash that is hoarded in various tax havens, they will simultaneously borrow in the US so that they can write off the interest for tax purposes.

Changes to US legislation in 1997, known as 'check the box' rules, also made it easier to avoid taxes on 'passive' income, such as royalties and patents. Under the pretext of cutting down on paperwork, US businesses were allowed to designate subsidiaries as either 'corporations' or 'partnerships'. If the category of 'partnership' was used, the subsidiary became a 'disregarded' branch operation and this meant that it was not subject to the global reach of the official US corporation tax rate. As the *Financial Times* noted, it created an 'accidental billion dollar tax break'.[39] The Irish state saw this development as a major opportunity to facilitate tax dodging and a host of tax measures were introduced to attract corporations that generated profits from royalties, patents and website advertising. A tax exemption on patent income was introduced; there were tax reliefs for acquiring intellectual property; there were other tax subsidies for companies engaging in research and development. The state also facilitated companies in transferring income to the Netherlands which became a particular hub for 'partnerships' that stored vast amounts of overseas profits. The *Financial Times* has calculated that €50 billion was 'reinvested' by global corporations that used the 'check the box' rules in Ireland.[40]

More broadly, Ireland offers tax dodgers five main advantages.

First, there are very limited rules concerning transfer pricing. These refer to a practice whereby multinationals manipulate their internal pricing structure to make it appear that extra profits were made in countries that have low tax rates. Until 2009, Ireland simply had no rules and corporations could artificially reduce prices of components used in Irish subsidiaries so that larger profits appeared to be made there. Limited legislation was introduced in the Finance Act of 2010 but it was designed to give legal cover to the existing lax practice. It includes a 'grandfather clause' so that arrangements made before 1 July 2010 are excluded from the new rules – provided they show appropriate documentation. As Deloitte put it in their tax planning pitch to companies, 'the presence of a formal transfer pricing regime should provide additional credibility for Revenue when dealing with (foreign tax jurisdiction) cases' but would not impose a 'significant additional burden' on multinational corporations.[41] The new law is based on an OECD concept of 'arm's length' transactions, which suggests that internal company prices should appear as if they were transacted between independent bodies. But as Michael Durst, a US treasury official put it, there are no 'uncontrolled comparables' to check if a corporation is manipulating internal prices.[42] It is even more difficult to apply 'arm's length principles' to 'intangible' items such as patents and royalties which Ireland specialises in supporting. The Tax Justice Network claims that the only effect of new legislative changes is to give a boost to 'auditing firms and law firms and economic consulting firms which derive substantial income from advising and consulting about those (OECD) Guidelines'.[43]

Second, Ireland has no 'thin capitalisation' rules. Companies may be funded through a variety of mechanisms, typically selling shares or through borrowing. A company which borrows heavily will pay a large amount of interest but one advantage is that this can be written off for tax purposes. Companies, therefore, often want to fund their operations through debt in order to reduce their tax bill. However, many countries have rules to prevent this type of tax avoidance – known as thin capitalisation rules – but in Ireland there are none. As a result, a holding company with nominal share capital is in a position to fund its operations by virtually unlimited borrowings and interest on these borrowings can be deducted for tax. Meanwhile, the directors can laugh all the way to the bank.

Third, there are no 'Controlled Foreign Company' (CFC) regulations that designate income from subsidiaries of Irish-registered companies as taxable in Ireland. In other countries, CFC rules demand that tax be paid on profits of a foreign subsidiary, even if they are not distributed as dividends. The absence of CFC rules is marketed heavily by the IDA when Ireland is pushed as a venue for holding companies. Subsidiaries of these holding companies tend to be located throughout Europe, the Middle East and Africa. The big advantage is that no tax is imposed on the profits, dividends or capital gains that flow in.

Fourth, Ireland offers extraordinarily generous support for wealthy people who want to take their money out of Ireland. A corporation can be formally incorporated in Jersey – where even more lax provisions prevail – and resident in Ireland for tax purposes. It can then receive streams of income from its subsidiaries across the world and pay out huge dividends on the profits. But these dividends will not be taxed if the person or company receiving them is resident in another EU state or one of the many countries Ireland has a tax treaty with.

Finally, a deliberate discrepancy has been created between a company which is incorporated in Ireland but tax resident elsewhere. A company can be registered in Ireland but have its central place of management located elsewhere in order to avoid Irish tax. It simply needs to show that directors meetings are held elsewhere, that the central decisions are taken abroad and that a majority of directors reside abroad. A search in the Irish Companies Office by the *Irish Times* for directors of Irish-incorporated firms found many were located in Bermuda or the Cayman Islands. Amongst the familiar names adopting this practice were companies associated with Abbott, Dell, Google, Microsoft, Pepsi-Cola, Sanyo, BMC Software and Novell.[44] Typically companies will have one substantial entity that employs workers and engages in genuine economic activity. But vast amounts of their income will also pass through subsidiaries which are incorporated in Ireland but tax resident elsewhere. The situation has become so serious that one Central Bank researcher noted, somewhat delicately, that 'a number of multinational companies resident in Ireland are utilising intra-group structures as part of prořt maximisation' and that this was showing up in flows of funds between Ireland and some rather unusual countries. The top two countries where inward and outward investment within companies flowed were Bermuda and Luxembourg, two well known tax havens. These two alone accounted for 29 per cent of inward 'investment' and 35 per cent of outward 'investment'.[45]

These measures have helped to establish Ireland as one of the premier tax havens in the world. There is now overwhelming evidence that corporations are artificially declaring greater business activity and profits in Ireland purely for tax purposes. Table 7.4 is drawn from evidence presented by Martin O'Sullivan as testimony to a US House of Representatives' hearing on tax havens. It illustrates how profits per Irish worker are exceptionally high – even when compared to profits made in other tax havens. US multinationals declare profits that are 13 times higher per worker in Ireland than in their worldwide operations. Nearly twice as much profit is declared per Irish worker than workers in other tax havens. Only Bermuda and Barbados declare higher levels of

Table 7.4: Profits and Profitability of US Multinationals in 2008

	Before Tax Profits (millions)	Effective Tax Rate	Profit as a % of Sales	Profit as a % of Assets	Profit as a % of Worker Compensation	Profit per Worker
Ireland	$46,337	7.3%	18.6%	117%	708%	$520,640
Switzerland	$16,352	11.5%	5.9%	141%	189%	$200,638
Bermuda	$8,354	4.8%	14.3%	132%	2234%	$2,610,625
Barbados	$4,4263	6.9%	38.0%	251%	11,218%	$4,263,000
Singapore	$12,255	8.1%	4.3%	84%	227%	$103,157
Five Tax Havens Total	$87,561	7.9%	10.0%	119%	417%	$298,334
World Wide Total	$408,720	35.2%	7.9%	42%	93%	$40,372

Source: Martin O'Sullivan, Testimony to Committee on Ways and Means, US House of Representatives, 20 January 2011. Based on data from Bureau of Economic Analysis of the US Department of Commerce. Data do not include banks.

profit. Despite the attraction of the latter, however, more absolute profit is declared in Ireland because it has the semblance of real economic activity and an aura of greater respectability.

Ireland's Tax Dodgers

The character of foreign investment in Ireland is almost totally shaped by the country's status as a tax haven. The main industries that currently drive Ireland's export strategy are chemicals, pharmaceuticals, medical devices and, to a lesser extent, high technology. Aircraft leasing also plays a smaller, though significant role, although this is often classified as 'asset management'. Yet it is precisely these sectors – alongside financial services – that devote most attention to tax dodging.

Hard evidence about the US's main tax dodgers came in 2004, when the US government introduced an amnesty to allow its corporations to repatriate their profits. Pharmaceuticals and medical devices corporations topped the list, accounting for $99 billion of the repatriations or 32 per cent of the total. The top tax dodger was Pfizer, which repatriated $36 billion in foreign earnings, and it was followed by another pharmaceutical company, Merck.[46] The next largest sector was computers and electronics, which accounted for a further 18 per cent of profit repatriations.[47] Half of all the tax dodging, therefore, came from the two key industries that Ireland's current strategy of foreign investment rests upon. It was not entirely coincidental.

Ireland has adopted a strategy of focussing on companies with an apparently high research and development component. The official explanation for this strategy relies on rhetoric about creating an information society. One official document, for example, baldly claimed that the country was engaged in a 'new industrial revolution'[48] but what few realised was that the main beneficiaries were the pharmaceutical companies whose primary aim was tax dodging. A number of techniques are used by the pharmaceutical companies to reduce their tax bill. Their crucial advantage is that they can claim that much of their product is based on 'intangible' knowledge, which is patent protected. Typically, pharmaceutical corporations transfer the patent rights to an Irish subsidiary, which can then demand royalty payments from subsidiaries around the world. The easiest way to do this is to claim that some research and development has been carried out in Ireland. The US parent company will, therefore, conduct most of the research in its home country and then – at the final stage – transfer some additional research work to Ireland. It can then license the intellectual property rights to an Irish subsidiary and gain tax-free income from it because, helpfully, the Irish government has written its tax laws to help this type of activity.[49] A special 25 per cent tax credit is available to corporations who undertake research in the European Economic Area and grants are also available to fund 50 per cent of the cost of feasibility projects and training. As a result, 40 per cent of Ireland's Foreign Direct Investment projects related to research and development in 2008.[50]

A number of examples illustrate how there is tax avoidance on a large scale. Pfizer sells 40 per cent of its drugs in the US but nevertheless claimed losses of $2.2 billion there in 2011. By contrast, it piles up $15 billion in pre-tax profits mainly in low tax countries like Ireland and Puerto Rico. This is a consistent pattern over years and reflects the company's strategy of using transfer pricing to reduce its tax bill. Similarly, Eli Lilly reports half its sales to be in the US – but in 2007, 80 per cent of its income appeared to come from a Swiss holding company that controlled an Irish manufacturing plant. Forest Laboratories makes one of the best selling global anti-depressants, Lexapro. But even though it sells in the US, it is officially produced in Swords, in Dublin. Strangely, Forest's Irish operations, which employed just 5 per cent of its 5,200 workers in 2009, apparently account for 70 per cent of its sales. Forest's Irish profits flow through a subsidiary in Bermuda to facilitate the tax dodging.[51]

The medical devices sector engages in similar practices. Boston Scientific, for example, is a large US company but its sales figures still show a disproportionate influence from Ireland. In 2011, for example, its holding company located in Galway was deemed responsible for 67 per cent of global revenue, or €5.8 billion. It declared $1.4 billion in Irish profits but paid only $60 million in tax – an effective tax rate of just 4 per cent. One of its techniques was to use a subsidiary that was not resident in Ireland for tax purposes. The company is currently facing two tax claims amounting to over $1 billion from the US Inland Revenue over technology licensing agreements within one of its subsidiaries.[52]

Computer and software corporations use a tax avoidance technique known as the 'Double Irish' or 'Dutch Sandwich'.[53] This was made famous by Google, which has reduced its overseas tax bill to a mere 2.4 per cent of profits. In 2003, the company licensed the right to its search and advertising technology for Europe, Africa and the Middle East to Google Ireland Holdings, which only had five employees. As it is an unlimited company, it does not publicise many details about its operations but, nevertheless, it is clear that it owns Google Ireland Ltd, which employs 2,000 people in Dublin. This latter company was credited with 88 per cent of Google's sales to customers outside the US, which amounted to €12.5 billion. Yet, strangely, the profits did not stay with the Dublin subsidiary, which reportedly gained an income of only 1 per cent on these sales. This is because it paid $5.4 billion in royalties to its holding company, Google Ireland Holdings, which has an effective centre of management in Bermuda. Irish law allows Google to treat this holding company as a Bermuda resident for tax purposes – even though it is incorporated in Ireland. This is rather convenient because Bermuda has zero tax rates while Ireland has 12.5 per cent. Yet it begs the question why does the Irish state connive in allowing a gigantic multinational to avoid its already low corporate tax rate?

As the Google example shows, the term 'double Irish' arises from the use of two Irish companies – one pays royalties to use intellectual property to another holding company, which then funnels it to Bermuda. The 'Dutch sandwich' arises because the money for Bermuda is routed through the Netherlands, because under Irish tax law there is no withholding tax if income is sent to another EU country. The US also turns a blind eye to all this, because the Dutch and Irish subsidiaries can be disregarded under its 'check the box' rules.

Microsoft pioneered this type of operation by establishing two Irish companies, Round Island One and Flat Island to perform a similar trick. However, when the *Wall Street Journal* revealed the practice in 2005, it reincorporated them as unlimited companies to prevent further disclosures of their income.[54] It is doubtful if Microsoft has dropped this practice as its pre-tax profits from overseas operations have tripled in six years while those of the US have declined. A US Senate investigation found that a subsidiary, Microsoft Ireland Research (MIR), paid $2.8 billion to its parent company in 2011 in exchange for the right to sell Microsoft products to Europe, the Middle East and Africa but received $9 billion in revenue. It was a clear case of transfer pricing to dodge taxes but the whole matter was disguised because MIR was, in turn, a subsidiary of the unlimited company, Round Island One.[55]

Apple pulled off an even greater tax dodge by using two Irish subsidiaries, Apple Sales International (ASI) and Apple Operations International (AOI). ASI acquired rights to Apple's intellectual property and received $74 billion in revenue income over four years. It only paid a corporate tax rate of 2 per cent on this vast sum. AOI functioned as a holding company for subsidiaries scattered across the world and, even though it had no employees, it reported a net income of $30 billion between 2009 and 2012. Yet it paid no corporate taxes to any government in this period. Apple has some economic activity at its

Cork plant but most of the manufacturing operations have left and been replaced by call centre activities. It is therefore a classic case of using Ireland primarily as a tax haven to avoid a tax bill of about $10 billion a year.[56]

Apple is not the only company that has achieved the holy grail of tax avoidance. The US software company, Novell, paid no tax on Irish profits of $315.6 million in the 16 months prior to March 2012. Another software giant, Symantec, paid no taxes on profits of $2.9 billion in 2007 and $742 million in 2008. The French equipment company Alcatel Lucent paid no taxes on its Irish profits of $313 million in 2008. The giant drugs firm, Abbott, did even better paying no tax on profits of €2.9 billion at its Irish subsidiaries.[57] Pepsi has moved its global holding company to Ireland and declared profits of $400 million in 2011. But it routed much of these through Curaćao and paid a mere $215 in tax.[58] This is an extraordinary pattern by any standard and makes a mockery of any denial that Ireland is a tax haven. It is all the more disturbing in a country that has assumed a mountain of sovereign debt because it took on private bank debt. Why, it must surely be asked, must its own population suffer so much in order to show immense tax generosity to global corporations?

More extraordinary tax dodging is to be found in the aircraft leasing industry. Ireland has become the leading global centre for this business as Irish-based companies own or manage 19 per cent of the world's commercial aircraft. The biggest leaser is a subsidiary of General Electric – a company that has an unequalled record of tax dodging in the US. It made profits of $14 billion in 2010 but paid no US taxes. Its extraordinary success, according to the *New York Times*, is based on 'an aggressive strategy that mixes fierce lobbying for tax breaks and innovative accounting that enables it to concentrate profits offshore'.[59] Ireland plays a minor role in this aggressive strategy through one of its subsidiaries, GE Capital Aviation Funding. In 2011, the Shannon-based aircraft leasing finance company recorded pre-tax profits of $765 million, making it one of the most profitable companies in Ireland. Yet it had no employees and only paid $379,000 in corporation profits tax to the Irish state. It used Irish tax laws to claim 'group relief' and so paid only 0.5 per cent tax on its profits.[60]

The IFSC

The centrepiece of the tax haven is the Irish Financial Services Centre (IFSC). Originally founded as a designated, low tax zone in Dublin's Docklands, it now refers to a virtual space for the export of traded financial services. Financial services account for 7.4 per cent of Irish GDP, making it second only to Luxembourg for the importance of this sector in its economy. The biggest category in the IFSC is known as 'asset management' and this involves very rich people putting money into investment funds that can be moved about the world to gain maximum advantage. It represents the purest form of capital, disconnected from any immediate tie to a local unit but, through its endless movement, creating a global rate of profit. These funds are organised through a threefold division of labour: *promoters*, who advertise and guarantee that the money is not misused; *investment managers*, who decide where to put the money; *administrators*, who carry out the low-key clerical duties associated with caring for rich people's money.

The investment managers are at the top of the food chain, charging a fee of 2 per cent a year and taking a cut of 20 per cent on the profits made. Typically, the investment managers sit in plush offices in Mayfair, London and use administrative companies to track the earnings and keep accounts for their clients.[61] Dublin's niche market lies in the lower level administrative companies and it functions essentially as the grunt worker for the speculative activity conducted in London and New York. Almost half of the IFSC's fund promoters originate in Britain and 39 per cent are in the US.[62] But even though it may have a somewhat lowly administrative function, Ireland has moved to the centre of global speculation by hedge funds. In 2012, €2,073 billion in funds was administered in Ireland, which was approximately 13 times the size of the Irish economy. Currently, for example, 40 per cent of the world's hedge funds are managed in Ireland.

The IFSC also hosts a considerable number of banks, which are free to set up 'special purpose vehicles' (SVP) or engage in 'shadow banking' because the tax laws have been designed to facilitate them. These mobilise funds – without public scrutiny and without guarantees to creditors – for use in speculation. Some of the larger multinational companies, such as Pfizer, have set up their own banks to engage in this practice. All that is required is that a sum of €10 million be brought together and there are few restrictions after that. The shadow bank needs only to make contact with an expert tax planner to ensure it claims tax breaks on interest paid on the borrowed money. As Matheson explains, 'no special rules or authorisations are required in Ireland in order for an SPV to achieve tax neutral status'.[63] The IFSC also plays an important role in the global insurance industry and has set out to rival Bermuda as a key offshore location. Once again the attraction is low taxes and regulation that suits business. Policyholder investments can be rolled over and can grow tax free throughout the term of investment. Irish-authorised insurance brokers can also underwrite business in other EU member states. And the Financial Regulator casts a favourable eye on the use of SPVs to engage in reinsurance.

A special feature of the IFSC is the tax provisions for Section 110 companies. Income from 'passive' sources such as interest or dividends should be taxed at 25 per cent but Section 110 companies are allowed to write off such a host of expenses that they are effectively tax neutral. They can engage in a wide range of activities from speculating on food prices or aircraft leasing or all manner of financial transactions. Although they are Irish resident companies they can be managed from abroad and so they are an ideal vehicle for offshore companies located in areas like Bermuda to have an 'onshore' presence in the EU. As Arthur Cox put it, Ireland is an 'ideal jurisdiction for locating onshore EU/OECD issuer with no tax leakage'.[64] Although these companies have a considerable amount of assets, they declare high paper losses to avoid tax. A study by the Trinity College Dublin academic Jim Stewart found that 75 of these Financial Vehicle Corporations had assets of €41 billion but paid no tax in 2009.[65]

Overall, the IFSC offers a number of attractions to those who want to increase profits by tax dodging. It is regarded as a clean, safe tax haven that lies inside the EU. Irish investment funds are virtually exempt from tax on their income and gains. There are no 'withholding taxes' when the income is distributed to non-resident shareholders. There is a network of tax treaties which allow tax advantages to be retained when the money is brought back to the investors' home country. The IFSC also presents an image as complying fully with EU regulations while providing enough 'flexibility' to avoid worries about over-intrusive supervision. A Qualifying Investor Fund, for example, can be authorised within 24 hours of receipt of the paperwork, provided the fund manager works through an Irish-accredited administrator. There are very few restrictions so that investment managers can borrow heavily to gamble and invest a high proportion of their money in under-regulated but more risky funds. Once an investment fund is listed with the Irish Stock Exchange, it can be 'passported' throughout the EU, meaning it can attract investors from across the continent.

Nearly 4,000 funds have been listed with the Irish Stock Exchange, which has developed a particular speciality in debt-backed securities. These involve claims on other people's debts, including the sub-prime market in the US. The Irish Stock Exchange is openly championed for 'reducing the compliance load' and even for 'providing a stamp of regulation for funds which may be domiciled in unregulated jurisdictions'.[66] Its light-touch approach to regulation is summed up by the absence of prosecutions for insider trading. Originally, the Central Bank was charged with dealing with 'market abuse' but then delegated its powers for a long period to the Irish Stock Exchange, which is a private company owned by stockbrokers. Lately, however, the Central Bank has been forced to take those powers back.[67]

The other big advantage is that state policy is shaped by financial interests, with the state acting as both a lobbyist for these interests inside the EU and constantly introducing legislative changes to facilitate them. Irish policy on financial services is effectively managed by the IFSC Clearing House Group, a body made up of top public servants and representatives of the financial services industry. It includes figures from Bank of America, Citibank, BNY Mellon, State Street and the Irish Banking Federation.[68] The Clearing House Group is not a lobbying agency because it is officially embedded in the key Department of the Taoiseach. It helps devise government strategy and advises on tax changes that are incorporated into the annual Finance Bills. In addition, the chair of IFSC Ireland, John Bruton, the former Taoiseach, promotes public lobbying for the IFSC. His position is funded by the industry but the IDA provides administrative support.

The Irish state's collusion with financial interests was in evidence when the EU Commission suggested a small Financial Transactions Tax. The proposal was for a 0.1 per cent tax levy on share and bond transactions and an even smaller 0.01 per cent tax on derivatives. This tiny tax could have raised significant money for the hard-pressed Irish exchequer. The EU estimated that €500 million could be garnered from this tax – the equivalent of what the government intended to raise with the property tax. Eleven countries in the EU – including France and Germany – agreed to go ahead with the tax but Ireland refused to. As soon as the EU proposal became known, the Department of Finance convened a meeting of the main corporations operating in the IFSC and asked them to make their case against it. No independent research was commissioned on the impact of such a tax on Ireland. Instead the state used material derived from a survey of financial corporations to come out vehemently against the proposal.

The reality about how the IFSC really works has been hidden behind a barrage of state propaganda that stresses its contribution to the Irish economy. Its supporters claim that it contributes up to 20 per cent of Corporation Taxes in Ireland but the official figure used by the Minister for Finance in response to a Dail question was that €630 million was paid in 2010.[69] That was from a total corporate tax take of €3.9 billion and so the IFSC's contribution, therefore, represented 16 per cent of all corporate taxes or only 2 per cent of total state revenue. Compared to the reported assets of €1,165 billion in domiciled funds that are invested in the IFSC, this is a minuscule figure.

Conclusion

The weakness of Irish capitalism is, therefore, self-evident. It has a shrinking manufacturing base that is propped up by foreign pharmaceutical, medical devices and high tech companies. These declare a high level for exports from Ireland but they also inflate the added value produced there for tax reasons. Suspiciously high sales figures are recorded for the US market and corporations indicate extremely high levels of profits for each worker employed. Ireland has become a service economy but, contrary to the official mythology, this does not indicate a shift to an information society. Indigenous Irish capital is still rooted in protected sectors while the development of a software industry has stalled. A key component of the Irish services sector lies in facilitating global companies in dodging taxes. This activity has helped to make finance services a key driver of the economy. Although the crash of 2008 arose directly from financial speculation, the Irish's state's economic strategy is to continue facilitating even more speculative flows for foreign multinationals.

Economic weakness has reduced Ireland to the role of a respectable tax haven in the global economy. The 'nod and wink' culture that is used to explain the venial culture of corruption in Irish society, therefore, starts at the very top of society. The Irish political establishment increasingly play a game of smoke and mirrors to create tailor-made tax loopholes for different segments of global capital. The state works in close conjunction with a vast, unproductive stratum of tax planners to keep abreast of the latest changes in tax laws and create openings for their multinational clients. Even though the IDA constantly boasts of jobs created by multinationals, the numbers employed are actually quite low compared to the needs of a growing population. Moreover, the dependence of a development strategy on the foibles of international tax law is extremely precarious. Up to recently, rulers in other countries turned a blind eye to tax havens as they connived with their own wealthy to defend their privilege but in more recent times other pressures have come into play. Increasing state debt coupled with pressure to monitor flows of money after the Wall Street crash has led to a new rhetoric that denounces tax havens. The current Irish strategy of development as an adjunct to a tax haven is not sustainable in the longer run

Given these practices, it would be tempting to define the Irish elite as a 'comprador class' who preside over a neo-colonial state. Ireland's elite, it might be argued, has deserted the task of national development and functions as a subservient stratum that acts at the behest of more powerful imperialist powers. There are, however, a number of difficulties with this analysis. For one thing, the Irish elite is not particularly subservient to just one imperial power but tends to hustle between the different power centres of Western capitalism. Their predominant connections are with Britain and America but Ireland's niche position as a tax haven is also used to establish connections with

German capital and even, possibly, Chinese capital in the future. The other reason why they cannot be seen as a comprador class is that there is no discrimination against native capitalists. The Irish state helps to articulate and coalesce a shared class interest between Irish and foreign capital. It supports foreign capital precisely because it does not undermine Irish capital. Foreign capital does not compete with native capital to sell its products on the Irish domestic market and merely uses Ireland as a tax haven for exporting goods and services.

The argument about a 'comprador bourgeoisie' also implies that there could be a better bourgeoisie that could undertake national development. It arises from a highly schematic view that imputes certain tasks to social classes before they shuffle off the stage of history. For the mechanical Marxist, the bourgeoisie has an interest in unifying the nation, establishing democracy and developing a working class that might eventually overthrow it. The reality, however, is that capitalists have no other interest than the grubby pursuit of profit and can live with a variety of political forms to achieve it. At an early stage in the development of their system, some embraced rhetoric of national freedom to win control of the state but that has long past and there is no serious section of Irish capital that can imagine another future other than operating as a junior partner to multinational corporations. There is, therefore, little point searching for mythical representatives of a national bourgeoisie or trying to use a nationalist rhetoric for service on the left.

The particular nature of Irish capitalism helps explain the state's response to the crash. After 2008, ruling elites were determined to offload the cost of the crisis onto the mass of people rather than the privileged. However, the Irish elite showed a very special enthusiasm for this task and never contemplated any sort of Keynesian response to stimulate the economy. Instead it led from the front in its embrace of austerity. It was one of the first to embark on wage cuts, arguing that exports to a revived global economy were the key to exiting the crisis. Meanwhile, it embarked on one of the most ambitious austerity programmes to restore 'confidence' to the financial markets. At no point did it even contemplate new taxes on the wealthy – even though the fiscal crisis of the state itself was one of the dramatic features of the crisis. And while the wider population denounced bankers and speculators, it deflected such rhetoric with talk of 'we are where we are' and promoting a general fatalism. It knew that financial speculation and tax dodging lay at the core of its economy – and nothing could be done to upset these sectors.

The future of Irish capitalism, therefore, lies only in being an adjunct to a gigantic scam to avoid taxes. A small stratum of society located on the legal–accountancy and tax planning nexus may get many lucrative opportunities, but this precarious position offers no long-term future for the hopes and aspirations of Irish society at large.

8

A Change in Political Management

'The Irish are a stoic people and they do their rioting in the ballot box.'[1] This is how the political commentator, Noel Whelan, described the outcome of the general election of 2011. It echoed a claim of former Fianna Fail Minister, Brian Lenihan, who boasted that his government had implemented austerity measures that would have caused riots elsewhere. The Irish have, it appears, a dignified approach and prefer to cause uproar at elections.

Ireland has a long history of mass mobilisations that focus on parliamentary change. Daniel O'Connell's Repeal Movement; the Parnellite campaign for home rule; the 1918 vote for Sinn Fein; and the Fianna Fail victory in 1932 have all been landmarks. This electoral legacy has left the country with an abiding fascination with official politics, and discussion about political parties, their personalities and local TDs pervade conversations. While identification with particular parties has weakened and most regard official politics as a spectator sport, canvassing by party activists is more intense in Ireland than elsewhere.[2] In the absence of mass protests, the 2011 election provided an opportunity for people to take revenge on Fianna Fail and the scale of the upheaval was astounding. A party, which had won governmental office for 17 of the previous 20 years, fell to third place behind Fine Gael and Labour, with their ranks falling from 77 Dail seats to 20. In an amazing turnabout, just one Fianna Fail TD was elected in the Greater Dublin Area compared to four from the hard left United Left Alliance.

The Fine Gael leader, Enda Kenny described the result as 'a democratic revolution at the ballot box'[3] but the limits of this 'revolution' soon became apparent. Fine Gael had opportunistically adopted an anti-banker rhetoric and framed the Irish economic crash as resulting from Fianna Fail's corrupt politics. Richard Bruton, for example, claimed that Fianna Fail had developed a political culture 'which ensured that bankers and developers were not dealt with before it was too late. This culture consistently put the interests of the insiders before the interests of the citizen.'[4] A more radical version of this argument was developed by David McWilliams in his play *The Outsiders*. This suggested that the country was run by a kleptocracy that helped insider friends. 'The idea is that in the crisis', he argued, 'Ireland splits not so much between rich and poor, or urban and rural or young and old – but between insiders and outsiders.'[5] Both the Fine Gael and McWilliams' versions denied there were inherent problems with capitalism, inequality or even financial speculation. Only a change in the political structures was required to create proper 'governance' so that markets could function better.

Fine Gael produced a policy document, *New Politics*, to address a 'broken political system that is at the heart of the economic collapse'.[6] It promised a ban on corporate funding of political parties; a whistle-blowers' charter; a register of lobbyists and new forms of accountability to create a 'fundamental shift in power from the state to the citizen.'[7] Yet, ironically, the actions of both Fine Gael and Labour in govern-ment gave the lie to the argument that all that was required was fixing the political system. Despite a rhetoric about 'new politics' and 'accountability', the old structures of lying, double-dealing and insider favouritism reasserted themselves.

Labour won its share of the vote by promising to moderate Fine Gael's right-wing policies. They would protect child benefit, oppose increases in student fees, stop attacks on social welfare, and tell the bankers 'it was Labour's way and not Frankfurt's way'.[8] Yet each and every one of these promises was subsequently broken. Fine Gael's mock anti-banker rhetoric came back as a parody on its own actions in government. When Michael Noonan was *opposition* spokesperson on Finance, he said that:

> What legal or moral compulsion is on Ireland, however, to honour in full debt incurred by Irish banks when there was no State

involvement in the arrangements? These loans were entered into freely by willing lenders and borrowers with absolutely no State participation . . . It is obscene that liability for these loans is now being transferred to the Irish taxpayer, in many respects to the poorest of the Irish taxpayers.

In the budget the (Fianna Fail) Minister for Finance reduced social welfare payments, punished the blind, disabled, widows, carers and the unemployed and he taxed the poorest at work, and for what? It was so that the taxpayer can take on liability for debts the country never incurred and arose from private arrangements between private institutions. What a disaster and an obscenity. How can the Government stand over it? [9]

This was fine rhetoric but when Noonan became a *government* Minister, he not only stood over the same actions but intensified them. There was not a better critique of Noonan as Finance Minister than Noonan as Opposition spokesperson for Finance.

A similar pattern was evident in the rhetoric about 'insider' favouritism. Despite talk of 'openness', the practice of appointing party loyalists to state boards continued with the same enthusiasm as before. Transport Minister Leo Varadkar, for example, made three appointments to the Road Safety Authority in 2012 – and two of them were Fine Gael members.[10] Justice Minister, Alan Shatter, appointed a donor to Fine Gael to a lucrative 'whistle-blower' post for the Gardai;[11] an election running mate of Taoiseach, Enda Kenny, was appointed as a District Court judge[12] while another appointment to the High Court had political and personal connections with Labour leader, Eamonn Gilmore.[13] The level of political influence in judicial appointments has long been so blatant that High Court judge, Peter Kelly, stated that excellent, potential appointees were 'passed over' in favour of those less qualified. The appointment procedure, he claimed, had become 'purely political'.[14]

The promise to break the link between money and politics has led to a series of window dressing measures. The Moriarty Tribunal Report had catalogued the circuitous route by which a $50,000 donation from East Digifone found its way into Fine Gael funds in 1996 just after the company had won a competition for a mobile phone licence. In his recommendations, Moriarity called for full disclosure of any 'relevant financial, commercial or other interests of the donor which may be material to the context in which the donation is made'.[15] If donations were over a certain threshold, he also called for disclosure of 'potential interest in government contracts' whether they were 'recently received, applied for, or where a decision in respect of same was pending'.[16] The Minister for the Environment, who had the power to act on these recommendations, was Phil Hogan. By pure coincidence, he happened to have been a fund-raiser for the Fine Gael party when Esat made its donation to the party and has remained a personal friend of the disgraced ex-Minister, Michael Lowry, who was the recipient of the funds. Hogan was also a key figure responsible for raising €3 million for the Fine Gael war chest to fight the 2011 general election. Yet both Hogan and Fine Gael refused to reveal the source of its €3 million donations or make any of the disclosures that Moriarity called for.

All of which brings to mind the oft-repeated injunction of the Sicilian aristocracy: 'If you want things to stay as they are, things will have to change.'[17] When a society undergoes such an upheaval as Ireland experienced after the crash of the Celtic Tiger, elites will invariably support a change in the political management team. They tend to adopt a new rhetoric, take some token measures and above all promise more 'transparency' and 'accountability' – all to ensure that things stay as they are. Far from being broken, the purpose of the political system is to align the interests of the corporate elite with the shifting moods of the population. Its structures are both adaptable to minimal change and resilient in preserving the status quo. A number of mechanisms work to create this overall effect.

Representative politics is, first, framed as entry to a privileged arena. Those elected to the Dail are cocooned into a wealthy lifestyle and enveloped in a political culture where there are no enemies but only friendly rivals. Politicians receive a basic salary of €92,000 a year but get a host of other allowances on top of that. They can enjoy vouched expenses of €25,700 a year; a dual abode tax allowance; a subsidised gym, bar and restaurant; free parking in central Dublin; free unlimited telephone calls; free postage up to 1500 items per month; VHI private health insurance and automobile breakdown cover. The political culture of Dail Eireann encourages a belief that politics is a 'career' where manoeuvring and backslapping are the avenues to promotion. Ministers get a €76,000 allowance on top of their Dail salary; a travel allowance that can be up to €1.14 per mile; and an extremely generous pension scheme that means their effective benefits and salary rises to the equivalent of €400,000 per annum.[18] This level of privilege puts many professional politicians into the ranks of the top 5 per cent of Irish society. While this provokes much justifiable anger, many miss how this privileged lifestyle has deeper political implications.

It encourages an unconscious identification with others who come from similar wealthy backgrounds. When a politician's lifestyle mirrors those of upper professionals or business leaders, they come to expect promotion and career opportunities as a natural part of their trade. Loyalty to hierarchy and fear of loss of privilege also become huge motivating factors. By contrast, their privileged life leads to an abstract understanding of human suffering caused by cutbacks in state spending. Politicians know the statistics and anecdotes that document the level of suffering – but they don't feel or experience it themselves. Public condemnation of their lifestyle also fosters a defensive attitude of protecting the political club from the tumult of criticism. No matter how bitterly one opposes other politicians, the social atmosphere of privilege helps to soften the edges and transform an enemy into a mere rival.

Ireland's 'broken political system' also presents significant obstacles against carrying through the democratic will. Democracy, it is assumed, only occurs in the immediate pre-election period but ceases once the ballot boxes are closed. This, it is argued, is the logic of *representative democracy*, whereby the population chooses those who will deliberate on their behalf rather than a form of *direct democracy* where they are involved in decision making. However, in late capitalism the disconnect between representatives and their electorate has grown to an enormous extent. Candidates can say anything before an election and then discard it afterwards, knowing they can normally retain office for the full parliamentary term of five years. Take, for example, the Sligo Fine Gael TD, John Perry, who got elected on a commitment that a cancer treatment ward in his local hospital would be opened within one hundred days of the government taking office. He even added that he would resign if that did not happen. After the one hundred days expired, however, he casually discarded his contract with the electorate and voted for government measures which led to more hospital closures. Without any mechanism to recall such politicians, it is difficult to see how representative such a politician could be. One can imagine an alternative system whereby politicians would have to reaffirm their mandate if (a) they voted against their own political manifestos and (b) if a significant proportion of their electorate signed a petition demanding a recall election. Such a system would, at least, put some pressure on TDs to actually represent their constituents.

Under the current system, politicians who break electoral promises are sheltered by the corporate and state media who present such behaviour as the very stuff of 'realistic' politics. Much of the Irish media is controlled by one man, Denis O'Brien, who has, according to the journalist, Anne Harris, intervened to 'pull' certain stories.[19] As a long-standing donor to the Fine Gael party, his media is hardly likely to challenge politicians who break promises. Rather as Anne Harris put it, 'allow a media mogul who has influence – O'Brien makes no secret of his desire for influence – with the dominant party and before long it may not just be the appearance of the dictatorial'.[20] Even if Harris' shades of dictatorship are exaggerated, the very organisation of journalism gives succour to the official 'game' of politics. Reports from Dail Eireann come via political correspondents whose source of information is personal contacts with TDs in the Dail bar and elsewhere. Just as security correspondents develop a symbiotic relationship with the Gardai, the political correspondents develop a similar relationship with TDs. This is mediated by the concept of 'balance' but this only means that politicians from rival, mainstream parties get a roughly equal, sympathetic coverage. Sometimes, of course, there is criticism but it never strikes at the fundamentals – how politicians will consciously lie to get elected.

Ireland is part of a wider trend across Western societies, which has seen a 'hollowing out' of the limited forms of parliamentary democracy. Mainstream writers such as Colin Crouch and Sheldon Wollin argue that we are currently living under a regime of 'post-democracy' or 'managed democracy'.[21] By this, they mean that while the forms of party competition persist, citizen influence over decision making is in terminal decline. Peter Mair explains that this occurs because both elites and the citizenry are withdrawing from the parliamentary process.[22] Political parties are no longer rooted in the mass organisation of civil society, such as unions or social movements but have become 'state actors' – offering themselves as office holders rather than fighting for any distinct set of policies. The more they become distant from their voter base, the more they resemble each other in a 'consensus' about how a country should be run. This means that official politics is increasingly driven by Public Relations machinery which, of necessity, relies on organised forms of lying to gain office. Parties organise focus groups to identify key issues for voters and then use advertising techniques to tailor their message to capture that sentiment. The 'promises' they stand on are only marketing techniques to gain the privilege associated with high office. Democratic decision making is further limited by the transfer of power to distant EU institutions, where corporate lobby groups enjoy unparalleled access to power. More restrictions arise from the growth of supposedly 'independent' institutions, such as Central Banks, which are immune from public accountability.

The elite withdrawal from even limited forms of democracy is paralleled by reduced citizen engagement. Voter turnouts are in decline, party memberships are falling and volatility among electorates is at an all-time high. The 'apathy', which many commentators lament, often arises from an acute sense of powerless rather than lack of interest. Vast numbers of people are tired of the lie machine that is official politics and, lacking an alternative conception of politics, retreat into their private lives. This mass 'apathy', in turn, leads to new challenges for political parties. For one thing, they require new sources of funding, both to sustain political machines and to motivate voters. Motivating disengaged voters means that ever larger sums need to be spent on colourful posters, media advertisements, sophisticated social media networking and straightforward gimmicks. Increasingly, these funds either come from the state or from corporate sources. The former source accentuates the pressures towards office seeking at all costs. The latter accentuates the trend towards new forms of patronage. Ireland's political system is a prime example of these trends. Fine Gael may present itself as a cleaner party than Fianna Fail but this is only because it did not hold government office for as long as its rival. When it held state office in the past, it behaved exactly the same as Fianna Fail did. The Moriarty Report found that Mr O'Brien made or facilitated payments to Mr Lowry of £147,000 and £300,000. It also found that 'It is beyond doubt that... Mr Lowry imparted substantive information to Mr O'Brien, of significant value and assistance to him in securing a Telecom's licence.'[23]

Parties like Fine Gael and Fianna Fail need a huge stream of funds to support their electoral mobilisations. They also need a source of patronage to motivate their activists. Fine Gael recruits many well-spoken barristers and solicitors to articulate its policies. But to motivate them for the hard slog of winning voters, it needs to offer subtle forms of patronage. The 'purely political' way that judges are appointed or the ways that the state's legal briefs are parcelled out to different firms of solicitors is influenced by this requirement for patronage. The older structures, which constantly reassert themselves – even as parties promise new politics, transparency and accountability – do not arise because of 'bad people' but because of the requirements of the political system itself.

These trends become even more pronounced when there is a weak form of native capitalism as there is in Ireland. Despite an image of the entrepreneur as the supreme risk taker, the Irish rich are actually loath to take genuine risks. As we have seen they prefer areas of natural protection or search out state contracts and guaranteed revenue streams. Public–private partnerships, contracts for public building programmes, contracts to supply state services – these are the favoured areas of investment. Fine Gael's stated intention of reducing public sector employment is part of a strategy of creating more opportunities for this form of private investment. But this intermeshing of corporate and state interests creates a natural arena for patronage. This is one reason why local branches of both Fine Gael and Fianna Fail typically contain a high proportion of small businesspeople who are not just there for policy discussions. Those at the upper echelons of the business elite rarely attend party meetings but make their own arrangements with the political elite on golf courses, social events or in the privacy of plush offices.

Far from fixing Ireland's political system, the Fine Gael–Labour government has simply slotted neatly into it. Whereas they once denounced the system as 'broken', they quickly found that the lack of real democracy was their best defence against public anger. Democracy under capitalism means that we get a choice once every five years about who the actors on the front stage are – but we are never allowed a say in the direction or the script. This elementary fact is covered by a distinction between the political and the economic. Choice is narrowly prescribed within the political sphere but completely absent within the economic. We may choose who the political representatives are but the very idea that the plebs might have a say in the appointment of a CEO is outlandish. We may, apparently, have a say in the political direction of our country – but none whatsoever in our workplace. As long as this dichotomy in decision making persists, corporate power remains inviolate. Big business and the financial markets will always bend the politicians to their will with talk of 'economic realities'. This is why a rhetoric about fixing 'broken political systems' may arise during a period of turbulence – but it is meaningless unless accompanied by wider changes that break the power of capital.

The Change

The shift from Fianna Fail domination to Fine Gael has, nonetheless, important implications for the stability of the Irish political system. Here we refer not to the policy changes or the desire of both parties to serve the needs of the wealthy but rather for their long-term potential to contain revolt. The global economic crash is producing earthquakes in the way official politics are organised in the debt-laden countries in Europe. Greek politics, for example, was once dominated by competition between the right-wing New Democracy and the social democratic PASOK, but both are being challenged by the fascists in Golden Dawn and the radical left in SYRIZA. In Spain, there has been a rise of nationalist movements while in Italy, a quarter of the population voted for the anti-political Five Star movement. Might such an earthquake be under way in Ireland?

The evidence of some change is already visible. The stability of Irish politics has rested on the overwhelming dominance of two right-wing parties, Fianna Fail and Fine Gael. The competition between them displaced a left–right divide and as John Whyte famously put it, Irish politics were 'without social bases'.[24] Support for these parties was originally based on civil war rivalries and party attachment was high, as it was often transmitted through family networks. The sheer conservatism of Irish politics was reflected in the fact that from 1932 to 2002, Fianna Fail scored an average of 45 per cent of the first preference vote and Fine Gael scored 30 per cent. In other words, unlike the rest of Europe, three-quarters of the population voted for right-wing parties and only 11 per cent voted for the very mild Labour Party.[25] This has already begun to change as Fianna Fail and Fine Gael now only command half of the electorate while a combination of Sinn Fein and Independents hovers somewhere between 33 per cent and 40 per cent of the electorate. In addition, party attachment has declined dramatically and voter volatility has risen markedly. Even before the crash, political commentators noted a collapse in long-standing partisan identifications, with Ireland standing at the bottom of a league table of Western democracies for the degree to which its electorate identified with particular political parties.[26]

However, while these trends portend major changes in the future, the recomposition of the Right is of even greater significance. Some have viewed the shift from Fianna Fail to Fine Gael as simply more of the same and, in the sense of their formal policies, this is correct. However, there are crucial differences in their styles of rule and this has important implications for the future. The Fianna Fail party had a unique record in Europe for holding government office that was rivalled only by Sweden's Social Democrats. Some conventional political scientists have explained this phenomenon by the reputation the party held for general 'competency' in government. Others have portrayed it as a near irrational phenomenon. Dick Walsh, who wrote the first book on Fianna Fail, claimed that at the heart of the party was 'a blazing mystique (which had) no social content' while J. P. Carroll argued explicitly that its strength 'lay in the fact that it drew on much that was beyond the 'rational'.[27]

The historic dominance of Fianna Fail, however, arose from populist politics that appeared to fit with the aspirations of workers in a post-colonial society. When de Valera formed the party in 1926, he described Ireland as 'an out-garden for the British'.[28] It was an accurate description of Ireland's continuing neocolonial status as some 97 per cent of its exports went to Britain and these were overwhelmingly agricultural. The party's aim was to change this agro-export model and, like Perón in Argentina or Vargas in Brazil, they set about constructing an industrial bloc that brought together workers and small capitalists. This meant a vigorous challenge to the big farmers and merchants who supported this trade and backed the Cuman Na nGaedheal government. The economic agenda of Fianna Fail has often been ignored because political scientists tend to focus on its formal aims, which were the unification of Ireland and the restoration of the 'national language'. However, Fianna Fail's anti-partition rhetoric never led to action and was only used as a symbolic totem to forge class unity in the 26 counties. The language revival campaign was effectively restricted to imposing compulsory Irish in primary schools and using the 'cupla focail' (a couple of words) at the start of speeches. The central aim of Fianna Fail was the construction of a vibrant, native capitalism and it sought to strain every resource of the state to achieve this. Crucially, it pursued a deliberate strategy to win a base among urban workers on the east coast of the country. This meant opposing the threat from the left and periodically invoking anti-communist rhetoric while promoting a view that the development of national capitalism was good for workers. In a letter smuggled out of prison at the end of the civil war, de Valera pointed to the possibility of class politics and advised his followers to 'lean more on the economic side' and insist on raising 'a national programme for the common good not a class programme'.[29] By and large, Fianna Fail was successful in this project until their eventual meltdown in 2011. They oversaw three major phases in the expansion of Irish capitalism and this, in turn, cemented their base among workers.

The first phase began after they took office in 1932 when they embarked on a protectionist strategy to foster the growth of Irish industry and used the state to develop the necessary infrastructure. Initially, this was a modest success as nominal capital invested in companies increased and industrial employment grew from 110,600 in 1931 to 166,100.[30] This enabled the party to make a shift from a reliance on a declining small farming sector on the west coast to becoming the hegemonic party among Dublin workers.

The second phase came with the 1958 turn when Fianna Fail dropped its protectionist strategy in favour of hitching the fortunes of native capitalism to foreign multinationals. It rescinded the Control of Manufacturers Act, which stipulated that Irish shareholders own a majority stake in companies. Some on the left – such as Noel Browne – regarded the shift as a sell-out of Fianna Fail's original ideals but this was to mistake the very nature of the project – to build up native capitalism by every means possible. The foreign firms that located in Ireland mainly used the country as a platform for exporting elsewhere and offered little threat to Irish industry. The grants and tax breaks used to attract them were also enjoyed by Irish capitalists – and, in fact, the latter received a higher amount per job created.[31] The modest growth of Irish industry combined with the influx of foreign investment allowed Fianna Fail to revive its hegemonic position over workers. Economic success appeared to lend truth to the claim that 'a rising tide lifts all boats'. While workers' militancy grew and support for the Labour Party in Dublin reached a high point at the end of the 1960s, it still didn't sufficiently challenge the Fianna Fail myth that what was good for Irish capitalism was good for Irish workers.

The third phase, the Celtic Tiger, was even more spectacular in its success and ultimate failure. It began fortuitously when the formation of the single European market encouraged US firms to seek a location inside EU borders. They initially chose Ireland because it was English speaking, had a relatively educated workforce with comparatively low wages and, crucially, a low tax regime. When the flow of US investment began to run out after the 2002 economic recession, Fianna Fail prolonged the boom by stimulating the construction industry. The long period of growth helped to shore up its voting base, which had previously shown signs of decline. The symbol of this period, the 'Teflon Taoiseach', as Bertie Ahern became known, did not have any particularly decisive or dynamic leadership qualities – he simply personified economic success. When the economy crashed, his mystique disappeared virtually overnight.

The long historic success of Fianna Fail, therefore, arose from its ability to translate the broad language of Irish republicanism into the narrower change of economic advance. It constructed a distinct 26-county economic nationalism that drew on post-colonial legacies to celebrate the advances of Irish capitalism and the coincidental improvement in the living standards of workers. It also forged an alliance with the Bishops and linked Irish identity to a deeply conservative strain of Catholicism. Flying the Papal flag became the substitute for flying the tricolour over the 'fourth green field' (Northern Ireland). Catholicism also offered solace when the ideals of 'competitiveness' and promoting Irish industry did not quite match de Valera's idyllic promise that the population would 'not merely be wage slaves or simply spend their lives making money for somebody else'.[32] Together, the twin pillars of 26-county conservatism, and Fianna Fail and the Catholic Church, held Irish society in a vice grip for decades and marginalised the left.

The electoral collapse of Fianna Fail in 2011 opens a space that has not existed since 1932. This is because the party had a real working class base and, within certain limits, its local representatives were in tune with the practical, day-to-day concerns of workers. At various times, the party rhetorically claimed to be 'a workers' party' or even a party of 'practical socialism'.[33] These claims were farcical but there can be little doubt that in the ten-year period from 1997 until 2007, for example, its voting base was stronger in the skilled, semi-skilled and unskilled working class than among upper professionals.[34] In general, this right-wing party was the majority party of Irish workers until the economic collapse of 2008.

Fine Gael shares the same right-wing policies as Fianna Fail but, historically, it has a different social base. Specifically, it has long had the reputation of being a 'socially superior party' with the core of its organisation located among the bigger farmers and, what a former leader, Richard Mulcahy, has called, the 'Ballsbridge[35] complex'.[36] The latter refers to urbane upper professionals who profess a more liberal outlook on issues of personal behaviour. From an early stage, Fine Gael was marginalised as Fianna Fail harnessed nationalist sentiment to mount a challenge to Ireland's status as an 'out-garden' of empire. Between 1938 and 1943, for example, the Fine Gael vote fell from a third to a quarter because it was seen as pro-British.[37] Moreover, many of the early leaders of Fine Gael – Richard Mulcahy, T. F. O'Higgins,

Ernest Blythe and Desmond Fitzgerald – were deeply involved with the Blueshirts, whilst others like John A. Costello and James Dillon spoke highly of them.[38] Subsequent attempts by the Fine Gael supporter, Maurice Manning, to present the Blueshirts as buffoons more than fascists are not convincing.[39] As the Blueshirts were growing in strength, the Irish Trade Union Congress (ITUC) claimed that it was in 'grave danger' from Fine Gael because 'their propaganda (was) a facsimile of the ideology of the fascist dictators on the Continent'.[40] The extreme right origins of Fine Gael and its support for the agro-export model meant it gained little support among workers.

Fine Gael's growth before its eventual triumph in 2011 can be attributed to two main factors. First, it repositioned itself to become more reliant on the 'Ballsbridge complex' by promoting a more liberal image. This began with Garret Fitzgerald in the 1980s, and while his liberalism was not deep enough to resist pressure to put a 'pro-life' amendment into the constitution, it was enough to allow Fine Gael to differentiate itself from Fianna Fail. Second, after its electoral defeat in 2002, it consciously set out to present itself as a non-ideological, catch-all party and modelled its organisation on its great rival, Fianna Fail. It changed to an ethos whereby Fine Gael TDs saw party branches as almost an encumbrance on their activity and built a centralised machine that carefully chose candidates. In the person of Enda Kenny, the party found the ideal figure to unite its urban and rural wings. Although he was the longest standing TD in the Dail, one commentator noted that 'Kenny had not been associated with any particular national issues – he had never taken a stand on any significant topic'.[41]

Fine Gael's triumph in 2011 arose because it was Fianna Fail's traditional rival for government. Many voted for it because it seemed to provide the quickest and surest way of ridding them of a party that seemed to have caused the economic crash. Polls before the election showed only a modest rise in Fine Gael's core vote, rising from 8 per cent to 14 per cent and so the key to its electoral success arose from its ability to attract the floating voter.[42] No strong bond was formed between the electorate and Fine Gael even in this historic election. One poll taken three weeks before the vote, for example, asked people if they felt very close to a particular party. It found that 10 per cent were very close to Fianna Fail and 8 per cent to Fine Gael.[43] Overall party attachment to right-wing parties has fallen dramatically, with voters developing an instrumental attitude of using one to remove the other.

Even as Fine Gael captured the 'floating voter' in 2011, its voting base was skewed towards the AB advertising category – the upper professional and business element. It won 41 per cent of this category as against 30 per cent of the C, D and E categories – skilled, semi-skilled and unskilled workers.[44] So even in its moment of triumph the party could not fully emulate Fianna Fail's success in transcending social class. Whatever voting base it had among the poor came mainly from its mock anti-banker rhetoric, and its subsequent actions in government rapidly disillusioned this grouping. Fine Gael's lack of a solid base of working-class support made it vulnerable to social upheaval if it tried to push through austerity by itself. Despite the tantalising possibility of governing alone with some right-wing independents, Fine Gael knew that it needed Labour to push through attacks on workers. And Labour, naturally, obliged.

The shift from Fianna Fail to Fine Gael has coincided with important cultural changes in the lifestyle of the Irish rich. Before the Celtic Tiger, the flaunting of wealth and social privilege was regarded as inappropriate. The wealthy sought to blend in with local communities, supporting the local Gaelic Athletic Association (GAA) clubs, attending the same churches and, crucially, sending their children to the same schools. The Celtic Tiger, however, changed all that. As mega-fortunes were made, the Irish rich embraced the cult of celebrity and ostentatious display. While builders and speculators led the shift, their hangers-on in the law, tax and accountancy networks were not far behind. One effect was a growing social apartheid as the wealthy developed enclaves that helped to bond them together and celebrated their success. The wealthy and the upper professional classes increasingly sent their children to private schools in order to achieve higher educational results but also to cement new forms of identity between them. Certain areas – such as Rathgar in Dublin – became much sought because they helped reinforce this privileged identity. The wealthy have always been more class conscious than the poor because they have more resources to develop their internal networks. But the Celtic Tiger dramatically accelerated their break from old-style populism and their embrace of a more visible culture of privilege.

One manifestation of this change was the way selection of cabinet Ministers came to resemble the British pattern. In the past, Irish government Ministers were more likely to have been educated in Christian Brothers' schools while their counterparts in Britain are likely to have attended Eton and Harrow. Not anymore. More than a fifth (22 per cent) of the current intake of Fine Gael TDs went to fee-paying schools. This was just one pointer to how the structures of privilege built up during the Celtic Tiger had important impacts. Only 8 per cent of the wider school-going population attend private, fee-paying schools so this stratum is clearly over-represented in the Fine Gael parliamentary party. However, the figures for the Fine Gael–Labour cabinet were even more dramatic as eight of the current 15 Ministers attended fee-paying schools.[45] It was a tangible symbol of a new style of political rule. Gone was the image of parties representing the 'plain people of Ireland' and instead there was something resembling the Celtic Tories.

Labour's role in propping up the dominant right-wing parties in government has also had a dramatic effect on the composition of its support base. In the past, the core of the Labour Party apparatus came from full-time union officials who represented skilled or unskilled workers. Unions like the Services Industrial Professional and Technical Union (SIPTU) – and before them the Irish Transport and General Workers' Union (ITGWU) and the Workers' Union of Ireland (WUI) – funded the party and helped provide the infrastructure which enabled it to organise. While Labour was never the majority party of Irish workers in the way its counterparts across Europe were, its voter base was skewed towards workers. But, again, not any more. The Labour Party's support base has become skewed towards the upper professional classes and, to a lesser extent, more skilled workers but it has lost out dramatically among semi-skilled and unskilled manual workers. The main reason for this change was Labour's record in government. Repeatedly, it has gone back on promises to 'break the golden circle' and joined with a privileged elite in implementing attacks on its own supporters. Sean Lemass famously denounced Labour for being 'the most respectable party in the state' and for being happy as long as 'they cannot be accused of being pale pink'.[46] It is a charge that has been borne out in reality and has now resulted in an extraordinary situation: a party called Labour gaining only paltry support in its 'natural' working-class base.

In response to this recomposition, the Labour Party increasingly profiles itself as strong on the liberal agenda. It promotes itself as a supporter of gay marriage and legalisation for abortion, but even here it sells itself short on these policies as it seeks to justify compromises with the conservative, rural element of Fine Gael. Meanwhile, Labour's embrace of austerity has left a huge vacuum for representation of the low and middle income groupings in Irish politics. How that will be filled will shape Irish politics into the future. But before exploring this question, we need to examine why the Irish have not been to the fore in protests against austerity.

9

Why Don't the Irish Protest?

S oon after the crash of 2008, a rumour went around that the Greeks were marching to the chant, 'We are not Irish, and we do not sacrifice ourselves for the rich'. As they marched on the parliament in Syntagma Square in Athens, this cry apparently swelled up from the assembled mass. But while one or two people may have voiced such a sentiment, there was no evidence that it was a popular slogan. This did not stop it being retold many times in conversation in Irish pubs as a way of contrasting the Irish and Greek responses to the crisis. 'What is wrong with the Irish?' many asked. 'Why are we so passive?'

Ready-made explanations were close to hand. Right-wing commentators tended to celebrate the natural conservatism of the Irish. 'We are a country of largely conservative law-abiding individualists who have little interest or faith in national government', proclaimed a columnist with the *Irish Independent*.[1] Others saw the Irish as the unwitting victims of a deadly combination of Catholicism and consumerism. Catholicism led to 'deference to authority and hierarchy' so that 'protesting against the status quo is stymied'. Consumerism produced a rampant individualism among the young so that 'protesting for collective issues is just plain not cool'.[2]

But there were problems with these broad, sweeping explanations. Catholicism and consumerism are hardly unique to Ireland and their deadly mix does not seem to have stymied protests elsewhere. Spain and Chile, for example, are similar to Ireland in this combination but have experienced widespread mass mobilisations. Some may suggest 'a post-colonial legacy' as an additional explanation but this will not work either because modern Ireland has had an important tradition of protest. The reason why there is no nuclear power plant in the country, for example, is because it was stopped by mass protests at Carnsore Point between 1979 and 1981. The reason why Irish women won even limited rights to receive information on abortion and to travel outside Ireland for terminations was because thousands engaged in militant protests. In 1992 they marched against a refusal to allow a 14-year-old rape victim to travel to Britain for an abortion – and overturned that decision. The reason why there have been no water charges in Ireland is because of a militant mass campaign between 1994 and 1996 which defeated attempts to introduce them.

Even when we enter the post-crash era, the question 'Why don't the Irish protest?' is wrongly framed. For the Irish have been protesting – and in very large numbers. At the very start of the crisis in 2008, 15,000 pensioners surrounded Dail Eireann and forced a government retreat on the withdrawal of medical cards.[3] The state had to change its 'communication' – or propaganda – strategy and approached further attacks in more careful fashion. More than 100,000 people marched in protest at the imposition of a pension levy on public sector workers in 2009. Later that year, 250,000 public sector workers staged a one-day strike and were about to repeat it when their union leaders called it off. The demoralisation caused by that defeat gave the government considerable room for manoeuvre and the protest movements dropped off. After a short period, however, there was a revival around particular issues. Protests against hospital downgrades have mobilised extra-ordinary numbers, with 8,000 marching in Roscommon, 7,000 in Navan and an incredible 15,000 in Waterford. Mobilisations against the cuts to disadvantaged schools; the withdrawal of personal assistants to disabled people; and cuts to home help care also extracted significant concessions from the government. Even more significantly, more than half of homeowners defied the law and boycotted a household charge.

The myth 'the Irish don't protest' is similar to the 'we are all selfish' mantra. When people are asked in an opinion poll if they live in a selfish society, the majority usually agree. But when asked, 'Are you personally selfish?', they disagree. The Irish have, in fact, engaged in quite a number of protests, but have not shaken off a mood of defeatism. One reason is that they do not have the language to articulate general grievances and possible alternative policies. They fight on individual, sectional issues but have not 'joined the dots' to create a substantial anti-austerity movement. There has been no equivalent to the Indignados movement that swept Spain in 2011 or even a citizens' movement that drove an Icelandic government out of power in 2009. Crucially, the presence of organised workers has been extremely limited.

How can we explain this absence of a generalised resistance, especially among unionised workers? Only the crudest understanding of the relationship between economics and politics would lead to an assumption that an economic crisis automatically generates mass radicalisation. In reality, political responses to an economic crisis are shaped by the manner in which the mass of people entered it – their experience of prior struggles and the existence or non-existence of substantial left minorities. Under one set of circumstances, the crisis can give rise to a near revolutionary dynamic, which if not curbed by the elite, can threaten their rule. Under a different set of circumstances, it can lead to paralysis and demoralisation. In this scenario, a longer period of time will be needed before there is a recomposition of trade unions and civil organisations that are capable of mounting struggle. Looked at from this vantage point, Greece leans more to the former situation while Ireland leans to the latter.

Instead of looking, therefore, for very general, cultural explanations, we need to examine the specific circumstances that shaped the experience of workers as they entered the crisis. Two factors, in particular, stand out. One was a pervasive ideology of what might be termed 'naive capitalism' which permeated almost every aspect of Irish life during the Celtic Tiger era. Another was the deeply embedded structures of social partnership which co-opted the leaders of Irish trade unions into serving the needs of capitalism. This culminated in the Croke Park process which aligned the union leaders with the state in encouraging compliance to cutbacks.

Naive Capitalism

The radical left has historically been very weak in Ireland. In Greece it dates back to the period when the Communist Party led a resistance movement to the Nazis during World War II. It grew even stronger after the Athens Polytechnic uprising of 1973 which overthrew an army dictatorship. Ireland's radical left, by comparison, was historically insignificant and its ideas have barely penetrated the workers' movement in any substantial way. The weakness of the left was further exacerbated by the apparent success of the Irish economy between 1994 and 2007, when the ideology of naive capitalism took hold among large sections of society. Although the left could connect with workers on individual issues, it was not able to challenge this pervasive ideology.

The Celtic Tiger boom led to both a rise in living standards and a growth in inequality. Its supporters focused on the growth figures for GDP and ignored the growing class divide. They treated inequality as a residual problem that was concentrated in the 'socially excluded' – a passive, minority category who needed help. Yet the evidence of class polarisation, which affected the majority, was there for all to see. In 1987, the share of non-agricultural incomes allocated to wages, pensions and social security was 69 per cent, but by 2004 it had fallen to 52 per cent. By contrast, the share allocated to profits, rent and self-employed earnings grew from 31 per cent to 48 per cent.[4] Yet despite this growing inequality, the Celtic Tiger was still experienced by the mass of people as a significant, historic improvement in living standards. The sweet taste of economic success was all the more savoured because of the memories of a previous era dominated by mass unemployment and emigration.

The growth in living standards allowed workers to seek privatised solutions to the failures of their society. One of the ways for dealing with a poor health service, for example, was to purchase private health insurance. At the height of the boom in 2007, 51 per cent of the Irish population held private health insurance. Although many Irish workers did not have proper pension arrangements, there was no demand placed on employers to make a mandatory contribution. Instead, workers were encouraged to seek individualised solutions such as private pension plans or purchasing a second home to have a 'nest-egg' for old age. The shift to a dual-income family meant there was a huge demand for childcare but as the state made virtually no effort to provide crèche facilities, costs escalated enormously. Many coped by working extra hours or – in what became the most popular solution – pressing family relatives to undertake childcare in the black economy. This experience of individualised solutions helped to prolong Fianna Fail's hegemony. The idea of well-funded, quality public services was scoffed at and instead individual 'choice' was trumpeted. With the connivance of the union leaders, a trade-off was set up between wage restraint and tax cuts for PAYE workers. Workers received low wage rises but this was subsidised via tax cuts. Although tax revolts in the early 1980s arose from resentment about the share of overall taxation contributed by PAYE workers, the tax cuts in the 1990s dovetailed neatly with the neoliberal paradigm. All of this helped to underpin a naive belief in individualistic, market-based responses.

Support for this belief system was pushed assiduously by the mainstream media and intellectual outlets of official society and it came wrapped in patriotic colours. With the rise of the Celtic Tiger, Ireland was finally seen to be taking its place among the nations of the earth. The commentator David McWilliams captured the spirit of the times with his veneration of the entrepreneur as a totemic figure of Irish pride. Here is his elevation of 'Robopaddy' – the Irish businessman in Africa – to the pantheon of Irish heroes.

> Ireland of the struggles shook off imperialism, forcefully allied itself with the anti-apartheid movement, ploughed a non-aligned furrow and generally painted an unimpeachable right-on image for itself. The financial counterpart of this was relative poverty and perennial economic underachievement that actually reinforced the overall package of post-colonial chic.

> Since 1990, and particularly since the late 1990s, the speculative wealth of the new Ireland largely built on property (here, then in Britain, and latterly on the continent) has given nice, funny, witty, decent, empathetic Paddy real commercial balls. Let's call the new wedged-up global Irish investor Robopaddy. Global Robopaddy is aggressively entering far-flung markets on leverage secured on decent property here. Robopaddy has the gut feeling of the downtrodden, combined with the bank balance of the overlord.[5]

This rather lengthy quote captures some of the main elements of the ideology of naive capitalism.

There is, first, praise for the entrepreneur. The negative image of the capitalist or boss was dissolved and instead the dynamic, go-getting entrepreneur appeared. The entrepreneur was a benign figure who 'created jobs' for the benefit of society at large. The Irish media promoted this cult of entrepreneur, suggesting that the population needed to pay them homage and express gratitude for their jobs. It interviewed the entrepreneurs regularly about their achievements and reported on the every word of figures like Michael O'Leary as if they were economic rock stars. Irish universities ran courses on entrepreneurship and business skills in their new centres of management 'science'. Entrepreneurs were invited in to speak to young students and presented as role models for success. Second, the rise of the entrepreneur was associated with national pride. Whereas a previous generation had been brought up on tales of republican fighters, the population of the Celtic Tiger years were encouraged to identify with Irish developers. These were figures such as Garrett Kelleher, who was building the Chicago Spire, the tallest building in the USA. Or the property developers, who had embarked on a 'Celtic reconquest' of London, by buying up its swankiest hotels. The *Irish Independent*, for example, ran the headline, 'Now the Irish are buying London – not building it'.[6] This form of national pride showed that, contrary to some romantic sentiments on the left, there is no automatic link between a post-colonial legacy and a propensity to rebellion. The memory of colonial oppression can be also be mobilised to buttress support for native elites – and nowhere more so than Ireland.

Third, Irish entrepreneurs were viewed as different to the other capitalists because they displayed a social 'concern'. Modern Irish society translated the older, cruder notions of the rich 'looking after' the poor into a new language of concern for the 'socially excluded'. 'Philanthropy' became the buzzword that allowed the Irish rich to make enormous fortunes and still gain huge social esteem. Many marvelled at the 'generosity' of J. P. McManus in voluntarily giving away millions – but few asked why he did not pay more in taxes. University halls and buildings were invariably called after living Irish entrepreneurs – O'Reilly, Smurfit and Sutherland – who were honoured as benefactors. Irish capitalism, it was assumed, had a kinder and more generous side because it was tempered with the memory of ancient suffering. Fourth, there was a sense of historic vindication. The centuries of fighting imperialism had morphed seamlessly into a celebration of capitalist success. The implicit suggestion was that Ireland had suffered for long enough – and deserved it. For all its embrace of modernisation, this ideology contained a deep and naive traditionalism which admired the Big Man who could ostentatiously display his wealth.

McWilliams' paean of praise for Robopaddy was matched by a more sober but entirely uncritical assessment of the Celtic Tiger by the academic establishment. Arguments about the growing inequality or the contradictions in Irish society were met with scorn. Writers from the Economic and Social Research Institute, for example, published a book in defence of the tiger economy, *Best of Times? The Social Impact of the Celtic Tiger,* where it was claimed that the 'housing system has performed well in the sheer volume of new dwellings it has produced' and that talk of 'strains and blockages' had been exaggerated.[7] The prominent historian Roy Foster argued that there were only two types of writings on the Celtic Tiger: Boosters, who praised it, and Begrudgers, who came from

the left, or from the nostalgic shores of neo-nationalism, part of their argument stems from a suspicion of creeping Anglicization, and a dislike of what an earlier age would have called rootless cosmopolitanism and liberalism.[8]

The neat alignment of the left and 'neo-nationalism' was designed to convey an impression that all that was modern and liberal was cheering on the Tiger. So cohesive was this uncritical intellectual consensus about the Celtic Tiger, that few saw its demise approaching.

This pro-capitalist ideology, however, contained a peculiar naivety. Capitalism was understood as a morality tale whereby the market rewarded those who worked hard and conformed to its rules. This message was repeated regularly on the airwaves by economists who became household names. The dominant message was that as long as Ireland played the capitalist game, it would be rewarded. The naivety was also evident in the way that the Irish miracle was conceived as a unique event. There was virtually no historic or comparative perspective which drew attention to the rise and fall of the Asian Tigers in the 1990s. Or to the epic 'surpasso' moment when Italy overtook the size of the British economy in 1987 – only to subsequently fall back into stagnation. It was assumed that Ireland's peculiar demographic advantages would guarantee prosperity and that as long as there were no 'excessive' demands it could continue for decades. Even when the crash was looming, many assumed there would be a temporary, 'soft landing'.

While the population at large embraced this ideology, it would be wrong to think that they were brainwashed because they did so in quite contradictory ways. The long Celtic Tiger boom fed into a new confidence to press for better conditions in work. An awareness of inequality produced a sense of 'relative deprivation' which stimulated workers to press for higher earnings – particularly in the construction industry. Occasionally, there were flashes of outrage over the inadequacy of the health services and many understood there was a contradiction between having a 'first world' economy and 'third world' public services. In more subtle ways, the embrace of individualistic outlooks challenged traditional sources of authority and helped to undermine the Catholic Church. Yet despite all these tensions, there was widespread support for the ideology which was promoted most actively by Bertie Ahern and Fianna Fail. This espoused a view of working-class ascent by playing by the rules of capitalism. Its central assumption was that if the wealthy were given the freedom to pursue profits, there would be a trickle-down effect for all.

The dominance of this ideology meant that people were unprepared for the crash of 2008. When it occurred, their whole framework for understanding the world was shattered. Many hoped the economic downturn was temporary and believed that if they 'kept their heads down' there would be some return to normality. Still others had a few savings and hoped they could use them to ride out the worst of the crash. Most of all, people were simply shocked and frightened about the insecurities ahead. Yet when they began to recover and sought to resist particular attacks, they faced another difficulty. There were few organisations willing to co-ordinate national action against austerity because the trade unions had opted for co-operation with the government rather than resistance. The long legacy of social partnership had come home to roost.

Social Partnership

Social partnership came into existence in 1987 and later evolved into an elaborate and dense institutional structure. The initial agreement between the unions, employers and the state, known as the Programme for National Recovery, was forged under the auspices of Charles Haughey. It promised union leaders access to the inside track on political decision making in return for co-operation in reducing public sector numbers and supporting wage restraint. The union leaders believed this 'political influence' would substitute for a strong Labour Party and would prevent the growth of a neoliberal Right. They pointed to the defeat of the miners' strike in Britain a few years previously as proof that militant resistance could not work. Increasingly, pessimism and defeatism about the mere possibility of struggle became their leitmotif. In the era of Connolly and Larkin, it was suggested, workers had to use 'muscle' to advance their interests but in the modern times, they needed to employ their 'brains' to develop a closer, strategic relationship with the state.[9]

Social partnership persisted until just after the economic crash and normally consisted of three-year-long national agreements. At their core was pay restraint but, as they evolved, they became ever more detailed about working conditions. The agreements contained procedures, for example, on outsourcing of public sector work or atypical working patterns. A number of unions, such as UNITE, regularly voted against the proposals but, as they were bound by the discipline of the Irish Congress of Trade Unions (ICTU), the agreements were imposed on them by the block votes of SIPTU, IMPACT and the Irish National Teachers' Organisation (INTO). The persistence of these agreements for over two decades implied a high degree of consensus between the union leaders, employer spokespersons and state officials. This consensus was forged through regular interaction at the National Economic and Social Council. This institution set the agenda for the successive rounds of partnership talks by stressing the need to raise productivity and 'competitiveness'. A key role in developing a shared outlook was also played by the Department of the Taoiseach which exercised considerable leverage on the participants.[10] From its core function in controlling wages, social partnership broadened out to become a fully fledged mechanism of rule for connecting the Irish state to its citizens. From 1996, a Community and Voluntary Pillar was bolted onto the process and an agenda of 'poverty proofing' was added. By 2003, the social partners included trade unions, employers, and farming organisations; seven voluntary and statutory social interest organisations; and the Community Platform, which represented 26 voluntary sector groups. This was now a highly elaborate structure for forging a 'consensus' between the leaders of civil society and the state.

Academic figures in Irish industrial relations and political science who wrote about social partnership suggested that it was a benign and progressive phenomenon. Hardiman saw it as a 'positive sum game' where both union members and employers made significant gains.[11] Roche argued that it was based on a 'political exchange' where wage restraint was traded for social progress and new mechanisms for resolving social conflict developed.[12] O'Donnell and O'Riordan praised the practice of joint problem solving and 'policy entrepreneurship'.[13] From these vantage points, there was no conflict of interest between the union officialdom and their members. Far from a diminution of union democracy and activism during the period of social partnership, the major unions, according to Roche, 'became *more* concerned with democratic engagement'.[14]

There are good grounds, however, for questioning this orthodoxy. During a temporary breakdown in relations between the unions and the state in December 2010, ICTU leader David Begg made a candid admission about the conflicts within 'partnership'. Specifically, he argued that union leaders now had 'an opportunity to reconnect with our own members, free of guilt by association with any aspect of Government policy'.[15] Unfortunately, ICTU subsequently resumed their cordial relations with employers and the state and the insight was forgotten. Nevertheless, it pointed to a fundamental blind spot in the academic analyses of social partnership – the gap that had opened up between the union leadership and their own grassroots.

At the start of the twentieth century, Sidney and Beatrice Webb, the historians of trade unionism, noted that there was a difficulty in the relationship between union members and the full-time official layer who dominated their organisations. Union officials receive a higher wage than their average member and enjoy economic security. They are not subject to the pressures and privations that come with working in a factory or office. They are often isolated from the membership and are not subject to regular democratic accountability. The Webbs argued that for these reasons they develop an abstract understanding of the issues they negotiate about. They may, for example, broker agreements on productivity – but are not forced to give extra productivity themselves. While many officials were originally motivated by a strong sense of social justice, their 'former vivid sense of privation gradually fades from (their) mind and (they) begin more and more to regard complaints as perverse and unreasonable'.[16]

The bureaucratisation of unions was also hastened by what Gramsci called the 'industrial legality' of capitalist society.[17] In modern society, the absolute power of capital has been limited by the rise of unions – but in contradictory ways. This primarily occurs through the growth of an industrial relations machinery which sets down rules and procedures. But these same procedures also limit the rights of workers to engage in strike action. They enforce a social peace in the workplace by getting workers to accept exploitation as a normal fact of life, while negotiating on its terms. The main concern of union officials is to maintain and extend this industrial legality. They believe their negotiating skills are the key factor in bringing improvements to workers. They, therefore, value stable relationships with employers as these provide an opportunity for displaying these skills. However, the condition of any negotiation relationship is that a certain trust is formed between opposing parties. Both employers and union officials must have confidence that contractual obligations will be adhered to. Union officials, therefore, tend to oppose the fickle moods of workers who fail to see the importance of 'adhering to agreements'. They are attracted to controlling and reducing worker–employer conflict and replacing it with 'orderly procedures'.

The wider membership does not necessarily share a similar orientation. Their primary purpose for joining a union is instrumental

– they seek monetary gain or improvements in working conditions. If these emerge through 'orderly procedures' they are satisfied but should the unions 'fail to deliver' there may also be considerable dissatisfaction. This divergence of interest helps to explain why the bureaucratic stratum in the Irish unions has been more enthusiastically committed to partnership agreements than the wider membership. However, the long involvement of the officialdom in partnership structures has helped to transform the union movement in significant ways.

First, the unions have shrunk as a percentage of the workforce during the partnership years. In the decade between 1994, which is conventionally taken as the start of the Celtic Tiger and 2007 when it finished, total employment grew from 1,221,000 to 2,143,000. But the figures for union membership showed a much slower growth and so there was a decline in union density.

These bald figures, however, hide an even more spectacular decline in key areas. Ten years ago, Dublin had one of the highest concentrations of union members but today it has one of the lowest regional densities, with only the West and Mid-West lower. Density is also declining faster among younger people rather than older people. Only 15 per cent of the age category 20–24 are union members and 26 per cent of the age group 25–34. More surprisingly, union density tends to be falling faster among manual workers than among white-collar employees – 45 per cent of professionals are union members, but

Table 9.1: Trends in Trade Union Density, Ireland, 1975–2007

Year	Membership	Union Density
1975	449,520	60%
1985	485,050	61%
1995	504,450	53%
2004	534,300	36%
2007	551,700	32%

Source: Roche, W. K. and J. Ashmore, 'Irish unions in the 1990s: testing the limits of social partnership', pp. 136–76, in G. Griffin (ed.), Changing Patterns of Trade Unionism, Sydney: Mansell, 2001 and Central Statistics Office, Quarterly National Household Survey: Union Membership, Q2 2007, Dublin: CSO, 2008.

only 28 per cent of craft workers and 36 per cent of plant and machine operatives are. While 35 per cent of Irish workers are members of unions only 13 per cent of migrant workers are.[18] This decline in density arose because the unions were not fighting for significant improvements. Once they accepted their role as social partners, they were seen as an ally of the political establishment and unable or unwilling to pursue major gains for workers.

Second, the unions became more concentrated in the public sector. In 2005, it was estimated that union density in the overall private sector was 20 per cent but in the key Foreign Direct Investment (FDI) sector it fell to a mere 11 per cent. Meanwhile it remained at over 85 per cent in the public sector.[19] The primary reason for the decline was that the unions accepted the state's priority of attracting foreign investment and made no determined effort to unionise this sector. Even if they had tried, they were constrained by the commitments given under social partnership and could not press for higher wages in this highly profitable sector. Employers had only to unilaterally match the low wage increases granted under social partnership agreements and then argue there was no need for a union. Even while the employers' organisation, IBEC, was claiming to be a social partner, its members were ridding themselves of unions. Employers in the FDI sector began the union reduction strategy in the late 1980s. In some instances, they operated a 'double breasted policy' where they continued to deal with unions in long-established plants but refused to concede union recognition in more recent plants. An interesting study of the phenomenon concluded that this strategy was influenced by management's expectation that they would encounter little union opposition.[20]

That expectation was not entirely unfounded because the unions failed to press the issue of union recognition on employers. They put their trust in a High Level group that was established under the aegis of Partnership 2000, after a major battle for union recognition in Ryanair in 1998. The recommendations of this group gave the unions far less than the Blair government gave to British unions. The British model gave mandatory recognition if a majority of workers sought this in a workplace ballot whereas the Irish model, by contrast, only gave 'shadow recognition'.[21] Unions could refer claims for improvements in pay, conditions or procedures to the Labour Court who would then decide if it was valid. In the event that it was, the Labour Court could make a legally binding recommendation but it could not force any company to engage in collective bargaining with a union. These provisions were codified in the Industrial Relations (Amendment) Act 2001 but even these modest measures were effectively overturned when Ryanair won their Supreme Court case on the issue in 2007.

The abject failure of the unions to organise in the private sector during the Celtic Tiger meant that many workers had no means to fight back against employer demands for wage cuts when the crash occurred. They were also pressed to accept longer hours, give increased productivity and agree to temporary workers doing the work that permanent workers had once done. The weakness of union organisation in the private sector also allowed media outlets – particularly those run by the Independent News and Media – to foment a private sector–public sector divide. Building on a sense of demoralisation and defeat, they targeted the 'feather bedded' public sector workers as the scapegoats for the ills of Irish society.

Third, social partnership led to decreased membership involvement in unions. Although partnership agreements were negotiated at national level, they included the detailed provisions that affected the working conditions in different sectors. In a rather odd form of industrial democracy, teachers voted on clauses which allowed for more outsourcing of local authority work. Similarly, council staff voted on the supervision arrangements for teachers. In reality, few people read the detailed terms in the 100 or so page booklets that constituted the partnership agreements. As a direct result, shop stewards at workplace level found that they were hindered from making advances, either by clauses negotiated nationally or by restrictions on making cost-increasing claims on their managements. Given these restraints, workplace trade unionism atrophied and union activity became associated with a small number of union loyalists who formed 'the committee'. Many of these became imbued with the view that employers were their 'partners' and ceased to promote struggle against them. As a result, participation in union meetings dropped and the layer of union activists decreased. Involvement in official branch structures beyond the workplace became even more confined to union loyalists.

Far from trying to reverse these trends and create more democracy, as Roche suggested, the union leaders used this disengagement to reshape their own structures. The primary purpose was to limit grassroots involvement and to base the union apparatus more firmly on a layer of loyalists. Elections for national officer posts in SIPTU were abolished and the franchise was confined to union delegates at a national conference. These delegates, in turn, were chosen from 'sector committees' where the general membership was not involved. Annual decision making union conferences were replaced with biennial conferences. Even the election of national executives was not open to the full membership but confined to those who served on committees. The result is a huge disconnect between a grassroots membership and a national leadership. The mass booing of ICTU leaders, David Begg and Jack O'Connor, at a large anti-austerity protest in November 2010, was simply a more visible sign of the alienation.

Fourth, social partnership has accelerated the trend towards 'business unionism' among the officialdom. This stressed the common interests of workers and employers over incidental daily conflicts. This type of trade unionism developed in the US during the McCarthyite era of the 1950s, when union leaders asserted that what was good for US firms was good for their workers. A similar realignment of unions with the needs of Irish business developed during the social partnership era. Paul Sweeney of the ICTU has noted that 'for unions and employers the biggest accomplishment has been getting into the heads of each other, to understand unambiguously what the deep concerns of the other side are'.[22] Unfortunately, it appears to have been mainly a one-way street. As part of the social partnership process, union leaders embraced the ideology of 'competitiveness' and joined the National Competitiveness Council. They encouraged workers to move away from older, 'inflexible' forms of work organisation and embrace arrangements which intensified work effort. They adapted to the main policy parameters of the state – even while rhetorically attacking neoliberal philosophies. They supported tax cuts as a subsidy granted to workers for low pay rises – even though it implied less spending on public services. Instead of opposing the use of public–private partnership schemes as British unions had, they embraced them – as long as workers in the private firms were unionised.

Social partnership was also underpinned by growing financial support for the unions from the state. Between 2003 and 2008, SIPTU and the ICTU received €4.5 million in training grants from FAS.[23] (The other social partner, IBEC, received €6 million.) In addition, €2.3 million was paid by the HSE into the account known as the SIPTU National Health and Local Authority Levy. Another €1 million was paid over by a HSE partnership fund designed to improve Human Resources in the health sector. This money was used to fund trips for union activists and HSE managers to the US, some during St Patrick's Day. These ventures were part of a classic management tactic to develop personal links with union leaders so that they could be co-opted to an understanding of the employers' agenda for change. One HSE official told the *Irish Times* that.

> Feedback from department officials. . . is that the visits. . . had their basis in wider efforts to improve industrial relations and develop a shared understanding of the scope for change and reform in health services.[24]

Another €790,000 was paid over by a local authority partnership fund to SIPTU to pay for participation in a training programme designed to garner support for public–private partnerships. Union delegates had previously opposed PPPs because they outsourced work to the private sector. However, as one local authority official candidly explained, the money sent to SIPTU allowed shop stewards

> to engage in the stakeholder consultation process on Public Private Partnerships (PPPs). The introduction of PPPs, she said, had become a significant issue for local authority workers due to fears about privatisation and outsourcing, so it was felt that investment was needed in training representatives to understand the issues involved.[25]

All of these developments, which occurred under social partnership, suggest that workers entered the economic crash from a very unfavourable position. The ideology of naive capitalism meant that there was not a significant minority who could politically argue for all-out resistance. Union membership had shrunk and had become more concentrated in the public sector – leaving many workers vulnerable to an employer onslaught. In unionised workplaces, grass-roots union organisation had been weakened and there was little experience of mounting struggle. Ironically, this left workers even more reliant on the very union leaders whose strategy had played a major role in fostering that weakness. Their own lack of confidence meant that little could be done in individual workplaces. The generalised attacks on their wages and conditions necessitated a general response but there was none forthcoming from a union leadership that had been shaped by a two decade long experience of social partnership.

When the employers withdrew from social partnership in 2009 and embarked on a strategy of pay cuts, the ICTU were faced with a strategic choice: they could have launched an all-out defensive battle or they could capitulate, albeit with some rhetorical denunciations. Nothing in their previous history prepared the union leaders for the first option. Moreover, they were perfectly aware that the stakes had risen sharply with the economic crash and that there was a possibility of a deeper militancy and politicisation that 'might get out of hand' if there were big battles. They, therefore, decided on the most tokenistic forms of protest – and then capitulated. The result was the first Public Services Agreement or the Croke Park Agreement as it was more commonly known. This saw the union leaders sign up to a reduction of public services numbers by 17,000 jobs – a figure set by the right-wing economist, Colm McCarthy in his commission on public services. They adopted the cliché of 'more for less' to indicate that with 'smarter' work patterns, the public services could do without these numbers. In practice, however, Croke Park 1 led to huge pressure on workers to give more in increased productivity by changing contracts, accepting new rostering arrangements and being willingly redeployed up to 45 kilometres from their workplace. More crucially, the agreement signalled the end of resistance to pay cuts, which had been imposed on public sector workers and which averaged 15 per cent.

The union leaders had hoped that their retreat would lay the basis for a growth in electoral support for the Labour Party and that their participation in government would bring them some eventual relief. However, when that moment arrived and Labour entered government with Fine Gael, they found that far from bringing relief, Labour Ministers wanted more. They wanted to reduce numbers in the public sector even further by between 30,000 and 40,000 and to get remaining workers to work longer hours. Every sign of weakness that had been displayed previously was taken as a sign that ever more could be extracted from workers. In an interview with the *Financial Times*, the SIPTU leader Jack O'Connor acknowledged that the Croke Park agreement 'took the best, organised section of the workforce out of the equation for social protest'.[26] It was an accurate description of what occurred. At the start of the crisis, the Irish political establishment made a strategic decision to maintain a shadow partnership process to help manage the post-crash structural adjustment. There were shrill cries from some of the right-wing press to break totally with partnership and slap the unions down. But a calculation was made that union leaders could be brought on side to help ease through a severe austerity programme. The collusion of the union leaders with the government via the Croke Park process became the key to social peace.

The depth of the crisis, however, means that this is not a stable arrangement. It is one thing for union leaders to sell wage restraint – when accompanied by tax cuts – to their members during a boom. It is quite a different matter to sell perpetual sacrifice when there is no real sign of economic recovery. The only way it can be done is through spreading a defeatist and fatalist mood among workers, but it is by no means guaranteed that this will be accepted forever. In the meantime, there are many who have already started to search for alternatives to the Labour Party and its supporters amongst the union leaders.

10

Are Sinn Fein Ireland's Radical Left?

One effect of the crash was to accelerate the rise of Sinn Fein. In the early 1990s, Sinn Fein was almost a pariah party in the South. Its members were visited regularly by the Special Branch, their voices were banned from RTE and its activists were vilified by the wider media. The overwhelming message of official Ireland was that they – rather than the British army or its loyalist allies – were responsible for a war that had cost over 4000 lives. Despite dropping their traditional policy of abstentionism, Sinn Fein could make no headway at the ballot box. In the 1992 election, they achieved less than 2 per cent of the vote. However, this has changed significantly as Sinn Fein took 10 per cent of the popular vote in the 2011 elections and became the second largest opposition party. Since then, opinion polls indicate that its vote will increase and, maybe, nearly double by the time of the next election. In all probability it will overtake the Labour Party in terms of support. While the charismatic image of its leader, Gerry Adams, has dimmed, he is still either the most popular or second most popular leader in the South. Other TDs such as Pearse Doherty or Mary Lou McDonald appear regularly in the media to produce cutting sound bites, tearing government policies to shreds. The shift in Sinn Fein from being 'a welfare adjunct of the IRA to the fastest growing political force in Ireland during the first half of the 21st century' has been remarkable.[1]

Their growth has resulted from two main factors. From 1997 to 2007, Sinn Fein repackaged itself as the most ardent advocate of the peace process, willing to compromise to reach agreement. By contrast, the Unionist parties seemed unwilling to share power and, according to republican sources, were supported by 'securocrats' within the British state. In a series of audacious moves, the IRA broke a republican taboo and decommissioned its weaponry; republican politicians joined police boards and urged support for the Police Service of Northern Ireland (PSNI); Sinn Fein accepted devolved power-sharing within Northern Ireland. The embrace of the peace rhetoric helped to dispel a Southern antipathy towards the armed struggle, but it also exposed a contradiction at the heart of the 'new' Sinn Fein. The Good Friday Agreement affirmed that the status of Northern Ireland could not be changed without Unionist consent and it resurrected the Stormont parliament. Sinn Fein had traditionally opposed both these propositions and at the start of negotiations declared there could be 'no return to Stormont'.[2] Even as late as the morning of its signing, party chairperson, Mitchell McLoughlin declared that 'Sinn Fein was opposed to an assembly at Stormont'.[3] The main concessions that Sinn Fein won were not in the constitutional field but in securing the release of its prisoners and a peace dividend that allowed former guerrillas to embed themselves in community organisations. Aside from these, it is difficult to dispute Brian Feeney's assertion that the Good Friday Agreement was 'a pale reflection of the 1973 Sunningdale Agreement that the IRA vowed to destroy.'[4]

The second main factor in Sinn Fein's rise was a left rhetoric it deployed, particularly in the South. Even before the crash, Sinn Fein used its outsider status to attack a political establishment that was mired in corruption. It presented itself as the voice of the most marginalised working-class communities who were left behind by the Celtic Tiger. After the crash, it developed a coherent set of policies which challenged the austerity consensus of the mainstream parties. These alternatives were framed in a 'realist' tone that accepted that the public deficit should be reduced to 3 per cent by 2016 – a parameter set by the political establishment itself.[5] This was to be achieved by taxes on the wealthy and a stimulus programme which helped to create jobs. The party advocated a 1 per cent tax on net wealth over €1 million with working farms, business assets and 20 per cent of the family home and pension pots excluded. It called for a third rate of income tax of 48 per cent on incomes over €100,000 with increased employer Pay Related

Social Insurance (PRSI) contributions as well. It demanded a cut in the earnings of politicians and the imposition of a pay cap of €100,000 on all civil and public service posts for three years.[6] It also proposed a €13 billion stimulus programme to create 150,000 jobs.[7]

These proposals have been advocated by left-of-centre parties in other countries but in Ireland, Sinn Fein stood out as the most vocal advocate of Keynesian economics. Its call to make the wealthy pay more tax was particularly popular among the manual working class. In the 2011 election, Sinn Fein scored nearly three times more votes among unskilled manual workers than among upper professionals.[8] After the election, there were clear indications that it was scoring nearly twice as much support among the former category as the Labour Party.[9] These developments – combined with Sinn Fein's membership of the 'hard left' European United Left/Nordic Green Left (GUE/NGL) group in the European parliament – led some to conclude that Sinn Fein was Ireland's radical left party. If Germany had Die Linke, Greece had SYRIZA and France had a Front de Gauche, then Ireland had Sinn Fein to represent views that were to the left of social democracy.

The suggestion that Sinn Fein represents a radical left formation draws on an apparent affinity between republicanism and socialism. If this connection is made on simply the basis of rhetoric, there are many signs that Sinn Fein leaders can employ a revolutionary left vocabulary on occasion. In 1979, for example, Gerry Adams declared that 'capitalist property cannot exist without the plundering of labour (and) we desire to see capitalism abolished and a democratic system of common ownership created in its stead'.[10] These pronouncements led academics like Ronald Munck to argue that 'Republicanism in Ireland cannot be reduced to an ideology of the bourgeois revolution: it has always had a radical component which has tended towards socialism'.[11] In more recent times, John Doyle has emphasised how Sinn Fein has 'a strong leftist, pro-equality agenda' and was 'an active participant in the "anti-globalisation" movement'.[12] However, the issue cannot be analysed in terms of rhetoric alone. Repeatedly in Irish history, Irish republicans have employed a left rhetoric to win a popular base and then used positions won to manage capitalism. Rather than simply focussing on left rhetoric alone, it is better to analyse the uniqueness of Sinn Fein within the wider spectrum of the Left to establish what its core project is.

The radical left, generally, favours an expansion of public ownership as a way of undermining capitalist control of industry. Some favour ownership by the existing state while others link it to a demand for workers' control. These tend to reflect a division between left reformist and revolutionary socialist positions. Sinn Fein's approach, however, is distinctive because its primary focus is on supporting private business rather than public ownership. Its specific policies to support business would not be amiss in right-of-centre parties in other countries. The 2009 policy document *Getting Ireland Back to Work* is a case in point. It does not mention any form of nationalisation and the public sector is only referenced for its potential to help stimulate the private sector. The document calls for 'support for Irish manufacturers . . . to reach an economy of scale, enabling them to compete with cheaper products'.[13] It proposes to provide R&D funding for 'Irish firms and entrepreneurs looking to set up manufacturing business'.[14] It wants tax credits for multinationals which source Irish goods and a major drive to attract Foreign Direct Investment from international firms in the renewable energy sector. It wants a 'venture capital fund' for native Irish capitalists to produce alternative energy products. The document calls for the creation of dedicated business and science parks linked to universities.[15] These proposals are variations on the current strategy of the political establishment which is to grant more subsidies to private capital. The difference is that Sinn Fein wants to combine these with a tax policy that targets high income earners and *unproductive* capital. Nowhere in the Sinn Fein programme is there any suggestion to increase the rate of tax on profits. This indicates that Sinn Fein's project does not lie in representing the distinct class interests of workers but in forging a common front with native employers to develop the national economy.

Sinn Fein is also unique on the radical left in being one of the best funded parties. One of the sources of funds is Irish America where the party is estimated to raise €530,000 a year. The funds are gathered via the Friends of Sinn Fein and come from various events such as lucrative speaking engagements or fund-raising dinners. Participants at a meal in the Sheraton Hotel in Manhattan, for example, paid $500 each to attend.[16] Other donations come from trade unions with Irish American connections and, crucially, from the corporate sector. Chuck Feeney, the owner of a chain of Duty Free Stores was a major donor in the 1990s while Coca-Cola donated $5000 in 2003. Sinn Fein's connections with Irish America also extend to right-wing politicians. One of its key allies is Peter King, who stands on the extreme right of the Republican Party. He was the main figure who campaigned for Gerry Adams' right to enter the US and later set up introductions for him at the White House. But he has also attacked Wikileaks as a terrorist organisation and claimed that 80 per cent of mosques in the US are controlled by fundamentalists.[17] The US flow of funds and the political connections with right-wing figures such as King impacts on Sinn Fein's activities in many ways. While Sinn Fein opposed Bush's war on Iraq, it refused an anti-war movement request to boycott St Patrick's Day celebrations with the White House.[18] It consistently welcomed visits by Bill Clinton as a friend of Ireland and was relatively quiet about his foreign imperial adventures. Broadly, the party takes a standard left nationalist position in supporting the Palestinian and Basque struggles but it increasingly does so by urging support for a 'peace process'.

Left-wing parties in most countries have been to the fore in defending women's rights. Sinn Fein has also taken up some of these positions, appointing a gender equality co-ordinator within its own ranks and periodically issuing statements on International Women's Day. But on the crucial issue of women's right to control their own bodies, the party is at variance with the broader international radical left. In 1985, a feminist current within the party won a resolution at the Ard Fheis (national party conference) to support a woman's right to choose but the year afterwards the leadership convinced delegates to reverse this. After the death of Savita Halappanavar in 2012, the party supported legislation to allow abortion where a woman's life was in danger but wanted it restricted to cases of rape, incest or sexual abuse. Sinn Fein spokespersons made it clear that they were totally opposed to 'abortion on demand' and what exactly this meant could be gleaned from the party's stance in Northern Ireland. There it joined with the arch-conservatives in the Democratic Unionist Party (DUP) in voting against the extension of the 1967 Abortion Act to Northern Ireland. In 2007, for example, they voted to throw out Department of Health guidelines to make abortion available when a woman's health is in danger. Speaking for Sinn Fein, Caral Ni Chuilin said 'My party supports the principle that there should not be any attempt to make abortion more widely available in the North'.[19] As a result, abortion law is governed by the 1861 Offences against the Person Act, which includes life imprisonment for any woman found to have terminated a pregnancy.[20]

These distinctive features of Sinn Fein arise from its nationalism. The adaption to a religious conservatism, the appeal to a wealthy diaspora, the articulation of working-class grievances alongside those of native capitalists are features common to many nationalist movements. The continuing appeal of nationalism in Ireland arises from the historic experience of colonialism and the uneven development in the world economy. No matter how much talk there is of globalisation and progress, capitalism is organised under the aegis of dominant nation states. As Nairn points out, this forces political organisations within peripheral nations into 'a profoundly ambivalent reaction against this dominance, seeking at once to resist it and somehow take over its vital forces for their use'.[21] Or to put it differently, parties like Sinn Fein try to mobilise different social groups to both challenge Ireland's role in the global economy – while remaining within it on better terms. After an economic crash in which the European Central Bank imposed a €64 billion bank bailout on Ireland, it is almost inevitable that nationalist movements like Sinn Fein will grow. The question, however, is will they deliver on the left rhetoric they employ to build their political base?

Lessons from the North

The modern Sinn Fein is a product of discontinuity and change rather than simply adherence to a republican vision that stretches back to the 1916 rebellion and before that to Wolfe Tone's United Irishmen. But from this tradition, Sinn Fein drew on one central belief: that brave minorities could substitute for a passive majority. The transformation of a mass civil rights movement of Northern Catholics in the late 1960s into an armed struggle of a few hundred guerrillas appeared to be evidence of this. When that developed into a 'long war', republicans became even more strengthened in the belief that *their* military actions were the 'cutting edge' that would bring Irish freedom. The justification for that war – even when it was unpopular among the Catholic working class – arose from a mythology that the 1916 martyrdom reawakened a passive population. Alongside this was a subterranean belief that the IRA Army Council represented the real government of Ireland in waiting. This tradition led to a strong scepticism about the capacity of the mass of people to take actions which could liberate themselves.

This is evident in how Sinn Fein has related to key struggles in the South of Ireland in recent years. When a €100 household levy was imposed, a mass campaign arose to promote a boycott. Sinn Fein refused to join in such a call, claiming the tactic was dangerous. When this was followed by a property tax, Sinn Fein again disputed the ability of a mass civil disobedience movement to mount a challenge. Instead they urged people to look to repeal legislation being introduced in the Dail by Sinn Fein. Whereas in the past armed guerrillas acted as the 'cutting edge', today it is the TDs in the Dail, but in both cases the capacity of people to act for themselves is downplayed. This also explains Sinn Fein's sceptical approach to broad-based campaigns. The party tends not to engage with such campaigns – aside from sending a TD to speak at major public meetings. Instead it launches its own party-based initiatives which mobilise very few. Nevertheless, these become photo opportunities to show that Sinn Fein is working *on behalf* of its constituents.

As the focus of change shifts towards the Dail, the question arises how will Sinn Fein enter government or more specifically, with whom? Increasingly, it is suggested that if the terms are right Sinn Fein can do business with right-wing parties. According to Gerry Adams, 'when you can do business with Ian Paisley, you can do business with anyone'.[22] The leadership refused to rule out coalition during the 2007 election and held open the possibility of joining one but the election figures did not work out. At the 2010 Sinn Fein Ard Fheis, there were two resolutions calling on the party not to enter government with Fianna Fail or Fine Gael. The leadership persuaded delegates to vote them down, promising a special conference should the occasion arise. Later Martin McGuinness suggested that they had no interest in joining with Fine Gael but this only left the obvious question: what about Fianna Fail? Eoin O' Broin, a key architect of party policy, has acknowledged that 'in real terms' the party's current position 'can only mean a future alliance with Fianna Fail, in a centre right coalition'.[23]

The break between Sinn Fein and the older republican tradition arose from its willingness to change policies and strategies abruptly. The party tries to achieve a constant upwards momentum by making bold changes, guided by the political context in which they operate. This entails dropping beliefs that were previously considered 'hard core', whether in the armed struggle itself or the use of hard left rhetoric. When the collapse of the Berlin Wall was followed by moves of the ANC and the PLO into the camp of the Western powers, Sinn Fein made its own strategic shift from 'the subjective politics of the revolutionary vanguard to diplomatic forms of manoeuvre'.[24] Its main objective became the construction of a pan-nationalist alliance. Whereas previously Sinn Fein had criticised the legitimacy of the Southern state, it now saw the Dublin government as a potential ally. If they acted in concert with the US and the EU, they could pressurise Britain to become a 'persuader' on the Protestant population. The party also argued that the Good Friday Agreement created structures – that if used fully – could help to develop all-Ireland institutions.

This pan-nationalist strategy has further accentuated their desire to get into government – if necessary, in coalition with a right-wing party. As O' Broin sees it, 'Sinn Fein in government in the North, and at a future date in the South, would place the party in key positions of institutional power from which to drive the agenda for reunification'.[25] Which raises a question: how would Sinn Fein's left policies fare if the party joined such a coalition in the South? The experience of the party's participation in the Northern Executive is instructive in this light. It points to a continuing use of left rhetoric even as its Ministers implement neoliberal policies.

One of the implicit agendas behind the Northern peace process was to reduce the size of its public sector and to create a low wage, low business cost base for foreign investors. In line with this, Sinn Fein agreed with other Ministers to accept 3 per cent 'efficiency savings' each year from 2008 to 2011. The effects were soon felt in reduced public services and a greater resort to privatisation. Sinn Fein's Education Minister, Caitriona Ruane, launched a policy for 'sustainable schools' and began a closure policy for those with fewer than 500 pupils. She also reduced provision for children with special needs and cut the number of teaching assistants. The teachers' unions estimated that at least 4,000 teachers and 12,000 support workers would lose their jobs as a result.[26] Sinn Fein's official policy was to oppose privatisation yet it made extensive use of public–private partnership and Private Finance Initiative schemes. These are a sophisticated form of privatisation as they involve the state buying in services from private firms. Sinn Fein's Regional Development Minister, Conor Murphy, transferred large parts of the water network to these schemes. He also went ahead with plans to meter houses for water supply despite promises there would be no charges. The same Minister also introduced the Transport Act in 2011 which forced Translink to both contract out bus services and compete with private firms for control of routes.[27]

Sinn Fein often claims that the gap between rhetoric and policy implementation arises from the North's dependency on the British Exchequer. Stormont Ministers, it is argued, have to work within constraints imposed by their British overlords and therefore have to make 'hard choices'. However, a similar justification is frequently used by Labour Party Ministers in the Southern government when they argue they had to take harsh measures because they are constrained by a Troika-financed programme. The weakness of this argument is also evident when Sinn Fein supports neoliberal strategies even when it is not constrained by external forces. It has led the way in calling for a reduction in the corporation profits tax rate to 12.5 per cent – the same as the South. Yet, as Richard Murphy has pointed out, this would lead to an immediate loss of between €200 and €300 million in Westminister subsidies.[28] Northern Ireland would then be forced into a tax dumping competition with the South to meet the revenue shortfall. Moreover, in areas where Stormont has greater autonomy over decision making, there is also little evidence of a break from neoliberalism. The Northern Ireland Executive had power to change the workfare proposals promoted by the Conservative Minister, George Osborne. Moreover, changing the workfare proposals would have been 'revenue neutral' – would have cost nothing. But despite verbal opposition from all parties, including Sinn Fein, all agreed to implement it.[29]

Participation in the Northern Ireland Executive has exposed Sinn Fein's economic policies to full scrutiny. A pattern has emerged of using a rhetoric that is similar to left-of-centre Labour parties while implementing neoliberal strategies designed to restructure the North's economy. Although the Northern Ireland Executive is composed of parties who fight over cultural symbols, they achieve a remarkable unanimity on economic policy. The Good Friday Agreement has, in fact, created an ideal terrain for neoliberal double-speak. Ministers designate themselves as the representatives of 'their communities' and compete for scarce resources. They publicly differ over cultural symbols in order to reassure their home base – and then agree on policies which disadvantage the poor. Even when there are rare disagreements, Sinn Fein never vetoes the more right-wing DUP lest it 'endanger the peace process'. Through these mechanisms, the party can play at being both the opposition and the government at the same time.

This style of doing politics was perfected by Fianna Fail in the South. It has long supported policies which favour the wealthy but, as a populist formation, it allowed individual TDs to oppose local cuts while never voting against the Ministers in government. Sinn Fein and Fianna Fail are very different formations because one is part of a corrupt political establishment – and the other is seeking to enter the mainstream. But despite these key differences, there is a remarkable parallel between the rise of Sinn Fein in the South and the early growth of Fianna Fail in the late 1920s. Contrary to its current image, Fianna Fail was once a left republican party whose leader, Eamonn de Valera, declared himself a follower of James Connolly. It advocated the replacement of the banking system with credit unions; it called for the replacement of army barracks with a citizens' militia; it supported strikes in foreign companies and often defined itself as the real workers' party.[30] It overtook the Labour Party by adopting a more left rhetoric, mocking that party's support for complying with the law during a land annuities campaign. Its entry into government also coincided with a global economic crash after 1929, which shook the foundations of Western capitalism. Yet Fianna Fail's left rhetoric soon disappeared in government.

Sinn Fein will not necessarily follow the exact same path, but the experience shows how Irish republicanism has had two faces – it appeals to the poor and downtrodden but it aims to unify the nation. It attacks the inequalities of global capitalism but it also seeks entry into its structure by leading an energised national movement. All of which shows why Ireland needs a more genuine and more radical left formation.

11

Conclusion

I reland certainly needs a genuine radical left – and one that will not repeat the betrayals of politicians who talked left wing in their youth and then settled into a comfortable Ministerial pension in their old age. This Left needs to offer a positive vision of a different society that is both practical and realisable. How can it come about?

The Left has to, first, see capitalism as an outdated system which causes untold harm. It is the most unequal society that has ever existed in history – worse in the distance it creates between rich and poor than that between Roman emperors and their slaves. Today three of the richest people in the world, Bill Gates, Warren Buffet and Paul Allen, have total assets of $156 billion, which is the equivalent of the economies of the 43 poorest countries that have a population of 600 million people. Some rich individuals lost money during the great crash of 2008 but many made a quick recovery. Sales in the luxury goods market – such as super-yachts, sports cars or caviar – have registered double-digit growth since the crash. In 2012 alone, the top one hundred billionaires added $240 billion to their wealth – enough to end world poverty four times over.[1] So despite a rhetoric about 'sharing the burden' which comes into play during a crash, inequality actually grows in these times.

Apologists for capitalism argue that inequality is irrelevant because the system raises the living standards of the majority of people significantly. This claim, however, can only be sustained for brief periods – during the 'golden age' of the long post-war boom or the Celtic Tiger. Today capitalism has become a crisis-ridden system that continually attacks historic gains made by working people. It has entered an era of counter-reform where it reverses policies which once ameliorated the lives of the majority. It reduces the share of a national economy allocated to wages; it charges for water, university education, access to healthcare; it privatises everything so that citizens, who once thought they had social rights, become consumers who pay user fees. The future it offers is extremely bleak.

The crash that has occurred in Ireland and the subsequent growth in inequality is part of a global pattern. Reforming this system to make it more caring is not possible because corporations have grown so big and have developed such sophisticated shadow networks that individual states cannot control them. About 147 super-connected companies have effective control of a large network of transnational companies.[2] These are bigger than many nation states and are capable of moving their money about the world easily. They are controlled by tiny, unelected Boards of Directors whose sole purpose is the expansion of their profit margins. Should any attempt be made to redistribute their wealth for the benefit of the poor, they will engage in 'economic terrorism' to bring governments to heel. They can sabotage a country through an 'investment strike' by withdrawing money from banks and businesses; they can run huge propaganda operations against left-leaning governments through their control of the media; or, in worst-case scenarios, they can work with their friends in the military to remove elected governments from office.

This level of corporate power means that Labour or social democrat parties have backed off from any effort to redistribute wealth. They argue that 'competitiveness' and 'profitability' must be increased in the private sector *before* electorates can expect any gains. Yet the more these parties give in to economic blackmail, the more the demands of the blackmailer become insatiable. Irish politicians have spent decades in appeasing the wealthy but this has only encouraged them to demand ever more. Not since the 1930s have employers imposed wage cuts – but, once they got a taste of it after 2008 – they repeatedly wanted more. A decade ago, no one dreamed that people might work for free as interns or have to work until they are 68 – but now it has become normalised.

A genuine left can only emerge in Ireland if it seeks to challenge capitalism rather than manage it and this means looking to Marx rather than Keynes. While Keynes debunked the idea that a market is self-correcting, he thought that the system could be stabilised by judicious intervention of the state. If governments increased spending and stimulated investment during a recession, capitalists would respond and get an economy moving again. But in the modern global economy, they might equally divert their money into financial speculation or wasteful investment in 'futures' products that promised greater returns. As the old adage says, you can take a horse to water but you cannot make it drink. Marx, by contrast, argued that it was necessary to take control of investment away from a tiny minority whose sole purpose was self-aggrandisement. The tragedy in modern capitalism is that so many aspects of our lives – the right to work or the right to enjoy a clean, safe environment– are dependent on a dictatorial minority who control the economy. The investment decisions of fewer than 200 bankers and developers in Ireland, for example, precipitated a crash and damaged the lives of hundreds of thousands. The policies of the Left, therefore, cannot simply be about 'stimulating' demand to encourage this tiny minority to invest – it must be about taking control of wealth so that they are no longer in a position to shape society.

In a post-crash Ireland, this means advocating policies which are practical but are not limited by a framework set by capitalism. These should address the needs of the working population rather than appeasing the demand for ever more profit. They should seek to bring jobs, economic security and a real improvement in living standards. The Left should advocate the following:

Refuse to pay off an illegitimate debt that was foisted on Irish society by bankers and the European Central Bank

The Irish national debt has risen to nearly one and a half times the size of its economy. It arose because the state took on the private gambling debts of the banks and, to pay for them, embarked on austerity policies which destroyed its economy.

Ireland should now write down these debts to a pre-crash level. That will upset global bondholders who bought Irish debt on a promise that its government would squeeze their population to pay them back. These include people like Michael Hasenstab, the California-based money manager at investment giant Franklin Templeton, who has already made a fortune because he bought up Irish bonds cheaply.

Equally upset will be the ECB who fear for both the contagion effect on other EU banks and also their own losses on the purchases of Irish bonds. But as it is not possible to satisfy both the bondholder–ECB nexus and the Irish population at large, the former will have to take the sacrifices.

Embark on an emergency public works programme to put
people back to work

The money saved from paying off bondholders should be diverted into a jobs fund. For every €1 billion invested in such a fund, approximately 100,000 can be paid at just over the minimum wage. Additional funds would be needed for capital investment to sustain these short-term jobs but overall it would still be far less than the current outlay on bondholders. There are many public works programmes that could lead to longer-term savings. There is a need to develop renewable energy as currently only 6 per cent of Ireland's final energy use comes from these sources.[3] There is also a need for a major housing insulation programme and remedial work on the water infrastructure. Building primary healthcare centres would also lay the basis for a shift to preventative medicine and cut down on hospital costs in the longer term.

Relieve mortgage distress; write down house values to 2003 levels
for those in financial need

If money is no longer being paid to bondholders, it can be used to relieve the distress that many families now experience as new threats of eviction loom. There is no need for a costly 'case by case' procedure or an army of financial advisors to tell people how to cut out satellite television or holidays to pay their mortgages. There could be a simple scheme based on transparent criteria through which people apply. If they make a full declaration of their assets and income, they should have their mortgages written down.

Make the wealthy pay for the economic crisis through taxes and nationalisation

Any move to stop payments to bondholders or to refuse payment to the ECB will provoke a reaction. Ireland may be threatened with being thrown out of the EU or there might be a withdrawal of funds from its economy. The corporate media play on this fear by conjuring up an image of the 'ATMs seizing up' and no money being left to pay for public services. This image is absurd as clearly the wages of workers continue to be paid via banks every week and, therefore, there is money in the ATMs. The issue, however, is how to cope with the flight of capital and wealth. The Left needs to take this threat seriously and explain to people that decisive measures need to be taken to counter these moves. It will be necessary to impose capital controls and to have strict penalties for those who try to evade them. Once these are in place, it will be possible to redistribute wealth to pay for a shortfall in revenue and provide resources for public works programmes. Many different measures could be taken, but here are some:

- There should be a 5 per cent wealth tax on all assets in excess of €1 million. This will necessitate the establishment of a comprehensive wealth and assets register.
- There should be an increase in corporation profits taxes so that all companies pay a minimum effective tax of 12.5 per cent initially and further increases where necessary.
- There should be a mandatory employer contribution to pension funds and an increase in their social security payments.
- There should be a Robin Hood tax on all financial speculation.
- There should be third rate of tax on incomes over €100,000 to reduce the Universal Social Charge for those on lower incomes.

Where businesses seek to sabotage these measures by closing down and making workers redundant, there will need to be further measures taken by a Left government. Firms which declare workers redundant or which seek to move production elsewhere should be taken into public ownership and forfeit their capital. Just as right-wing governments have been prepared to rewrite laws and do everything to impose cuts on the majority, so too must a Left government be willing to take whatever measures are necessary to safeguard the living standards of its people.

Take Ireland's natural resources into public ownership

In the past, many school students learnt that Ireland had few natural resources. All the current available evidence, however, suggests that this is not so. Ireland's offshore territory consists of 635,000km^2 – nine times the size of the country – and the Atlantic margin may contain a potential 10 billion barrels of oil or gas. The latter figure comes from a 2006 report of the Department of Communications, Energy and Natural Resources and, if true, the value is approximately €420 billion.[4] Even if the figure was somewhat exaggerated in order to attract prospecting companies, it still leaves Ireland holding a very valuable resource. Currently, the total government take – the combination of taxes, royalties and bonus income – from these reserves is minimal. A study of 45 fiscal systems for natural resources by the petroleum consultant Daniel Johnston shows that Ireland has the lowest returns of all the countries studied.[5] The Irish state itself has boasted that 'Ireland has had the best fiscal terms in the world for exploration and production'.[6]

Ireland needs to take control of these resources and declare that these reserves are the property of its people. Existing contracts with oil and gas companies need to be revoked as they were negotiated under terms set by former Fianna Fail Ministers, Ray Burke and Bertie Ahern. Once this occurs, the state can deploy a variety of mechanisms to both raise capital and access technical expertise needed to extract reserves from the sea bed. It can have production-sharing agreements or service contracts with global corporations or it can co-operate with other countries that have adopted a left nationalist approach to gain expertise – or do both. There is no reason why it cannot follow an example set by Norway which achieves a 75 per cent government take from its reserves.

Adopt a development strategy based on public ownership and workers' control

State agencies continually boast about the level of foreign investment that is 'attracted' to Ireland and suggest that it gets more jobs per head of population from this source than other countries. This foreign investment, which is concentrated in manufacturing exports and internationally traded services, accounts for just 7 per cent of those employed. It is also increasingly precarious as much of it is based on Ireland's status as a tax haven. In the longer term, it does not lay the basis for a development strategy that will free Ireland from the scourge of forced emigration. Nor will a shift to subsidising indigenous capitalists deliver needed employment. The Irish state deployed this strategy for decades and it still could not provide jobs for its people.

An alternative strategy of using public sector investment is required. There needs to be a halt to the privatisation of Irish semi-state companies and they should be encouraged to expand. Instead of selling off harvesting rights to Coillte, for example, the company should extend its activities into the area of renewable energy. There is also a need for state investment into areas where Irish capitalists have feared to tread. Irish workers have built up a considerable expertise in the pharmaceutical industries. If, and probably when, there is a withdrawal by multinationals from this sector, there will be a need for state industries to produce generic drugs.

At the moment, state-owned companies are managed by people who aspire to be directors in the private sector and who are the prime advocates of privatisation. The more they attack workers' conditions and deprive them of a real say in their companies, the more 'commercially successful' they think they are. Yet genuine workers' involvement – and, indeed, self-management – is the key to stopping both bureaucratisation and the lure of private profit. Far from hindering efficiency, workers' control enhances it by engaging with the creative energies of the majority of employees rather than the supposed brilliance of a few managers.

Can the Left Do It?

These policies are practical but anti-capitalist. They are realistic – but not utopian. They should not, however, be seen as simply governmental policies but demands that can be counterposed to pressures for more austerity.

The great dilemma of the modern age is fatalism. Many know that capitalism is a failing system but they believe that alternative policies are not 'in the real world'. This arises because people have little belief in their own capacity to confront the rapacious power of the wealthy. There are understandable reasons for this feeling. The betrayals of the workers' movement by Stalinist and social democratic parties have left many rudderless. Moreover, the old methods, which were once advocated by these parties, of using the state apparatus to tame corporations are less possible. A new method of bringing change is required – one that encourages mass mobilisation from below. But many have grown up in a period where there have been few such movements that were able to wrestle real reforms from powerful elites. We are therefore caught between two worlds – between the decline of top-down politics and the birth of a new grassroots politics. As well as proposing policy alternatives, the Left needs to devote much energy to showing *how* they can be achieved.

Here we come to the difference between an approach that seeks to reform capitalism through capturing governmental office – and one that seeks its revolutionary overthrow. Let us assume for the moment that a left-wing government was elected in Ireland or, in the immediate period, Greece through the rise of SYRIZA. Such a government, which proposed policies similar to those outlined above, would both terrify the rich and raise the confidence and aspirations of workers. In other words, it would raise the conflict between the social classes to its highest point. It is doubtful in such a situation if the energies of a hundred or so parliamentarians could exert full command over the state apparatus. Top civil servants, judges, army officers, who have all been drawn from the upper classes, would be unlikely to energetically pursue policies which strip their own class of much of their wealth. More broadly, such a government would face immense economic blackmail from institutions such as the EU or the anonymous 'market forces'. The choice facing such a government would be to retreat – or move beyond the confines set by existing political structures.

The reality is that no serious challenge to the power of capitalists is possible without the mobilisation of the immense majority of people. The old model of looking to representatives in the parliament to act on behalf of a passive majority can never defeat the insidious power of money. People need to rebel themselves – to demonstrate on the streets; to occupy their workplaces; to stage general stoppages and to develop their own organs of counter-power. These will consist of assemblies in workplaces and neighbourhoods where people come together to democratically decide on actions. Before there can be any real change in Ireland, there will have to be a break with the idea that a brave minority or a few deputies in the Dail can change life for the mass of people. Instead of 'giving out' on the popular Joe Duffy talk show, there will have to be a new ethos of democratic self-organisation. Linked with this, and crucial to its development, there will need to be a clean-out of the Labour Party dominance of Irish unions. This is the only way to return to workers' organisations that are willing and capable of struggling for their members.

Can the Irish Left Promote This New Method of Bringing Change and Gain Support for It?

There already exist well organised far left parties in the shape of the Socialist Workers Party and the Socialist Party. For two decades, both have played credible roles in single issue campaigns and have developed a well educated political membership. But to make gains in the new situation, a broad radical left organisation also needs to emerge to unite these elements with far wider layers of people. The first attempt to do so, the United Left Alliance (ULA), showed what was possible when five TDs were elected to the Dail. Many attended a round of public meetings across the country and expressed enthusiasm from the project. At one of its first meetings, Joe Higgins TD proclaimed that the Irish left had gone past the joke of Brendan Behan – that its first item would be a split.

Unfortunately, the joke came back to haunt the ULA. One TD, Seamus Healy, left because the ULA did not call for the resignation of

Mick Wallace, the businessman-turned-politician, after he admitted cheating on taxes. Then the Socialist Party left, declaring that the ULA 'was no longer a principled left alliance'.[7] They had not called for the resignation of Mick Wallace but were concerned about the political association that their former member, Clare Daly, had with Wallace. Others were concerned that the very existence of revolutionary organisations was a hindrance. In reality, these objections reflected a failure to understand that there can be diversity within a left alliance. The problems, in fact, lay elsewhere. The ULA combined an obsession with elections with an undemocratic internal regime based on competing blocks. It failed to develop coherent strategies for launching mass campaigns and intervening within them to promote a common position. It remained primarily an electoral front based on talented individuals.

Despite these failures, there is a need for both a broad, radical left alliance and revolutionary socialist organisations. The first attempt to create such an alliance stumbled but lessons can be drawn. The most crucial is that the Left needs to leave the lonely, but cosy, world of the fringes and develop a style of speaking and forms of organisation that creates a space for new layers of people who are being politicised by the crisis. There is a need for theory and political education that illuminates how capitalism works but this will not be developed by keyboard warriors or Facebook fighters who polemicise with each other from the privacy of their bedrooms. A real understanding of how the current system works demands some serious study. It is not a matter of learning off a few quotations from sacred texts but discovering the genuine insights of writers like Marx and applying them to the twenty-first century. There is also a need to convey these insights to those who are most prepared to use them – people who want to resist and fight.

A broad, radical left must arise with, and draw its energies from, larger social movements. This is not to imply that a radical left party and a social movement are synonymous. A social movement needs to be open enough to draw in people of different backgrounds and policies. A radical left party is necessarily narrower as it has to win people to a distinct socialist position. Nevertheless, a radical left can emerge from the key activists in social movements who have become convinced by their own experience of the need for socialist politics.

Important anti-austerity movements have begun to emerge in Ireland through fights against the property taxes and water charges. The first sign of workers' dissatisfaction with compromising union leaders has also become visible. A key strategic goal of a radical left must be to link the militancy of radicalised social movements to the organised power of workers. Focussing on this will also take the radical left far beyond an electoralist outlook, which sees the winning of Dail seats as the primary goal. This will also help restore a democratic ethos to the Left because the focus will not be on political representatives but the wider energy and determination of the movement from below. Dail TDs should only ever be viewed as the voice of a wider movement and need to be subjected to democratic accountability. This, ultimately, is one way to avoid the betrayals that come with the notion of politics as a career culminating in Ministerial office.

The People Before Profit Alliance has begun the task of creating a broad radical left. It speaks the language of a twenty-first-century movement and is built around campaigning activity. It does not demand political purity from its members but accepts diversity in its ranks. It links those who want openly revolutionary change with those who want to fight for real reforms. It is above all a space where new activists can join the dots between the many individual battles that are breaking out against capitalism. The coming years will tell whether it can spearhead a campaign to develop a large and substantial Left in Ireland. The conditions for doing so have never been more opportune – we need to seize the time.

Notes

Website addresses cited in this publication were checked on 22 March 2013.

Chapter 1

1   'Chief struggles to revive Merrill Lynch', *New York Times*, 18 July 2008.
2   'When Irish eyes are crying', *Vanity Fair*, March 2011.
3   Memorandum from Merrill Lynch 28 September 2009, p. 2. www. oireachtas.ie/documents/committees30thdail/pac/reports/documents regruarantee/document3.pdf
4   Memorandum from Merrill Lynch, 28 September 2009, p. 9.
5   Memorandum from Merrill Lynch, 28 September 2009, p. 7.
6   'A worthwhile project', *Finance magazine.Com*, March 2004.
7   'McCann corners Ireland's asset-covered bond market', *The Lawyer.com*, 24 April 2004.
8   EU Commission, 'The Economic Adjustment Programme for Ireland', *Occasional Paper 76*, 2011, p. 9.
9   'Main law firms' dominance pays off handsomely', *Irish Times*, 10 May 2010.
10 Dáil Éireann Debates, Vol. 755, No. 1, Written Answers No 68: Consultancy Contracts, 9 February 2012.
11 Ibid.
12 'Nama runs up €27.5 million legal bill in two years', *Irish Times*, 8 February 2012.
13 Public Accounts Committee Documents – Transcript of Handwritten Note of Meeting with Goldman Sachs and Department, Central Bank and Financial Regulator, 21 September 2008.
14 'Erin go broke' *New York Times*, 19 April 2009.
15 www.youtube.com/watch?v=EmJNL1BmukU
16 Dáil Éireann Debates, Vol. 662, No. 1, Debates on Credit Institution (Financial Support Bill), 30 September 2008.
17 Ibid.
18 'Nationalisation has "downsides"', *Irish Times*, 4 April 2009.

19 NTMA Debt Projections. www.ntma.ie/business-areas/funding-and-debt-management/debt-profile/debt-projections/

20 National Pension Reserve Fund Quarterly Performance and Portfolio Update, 30 September 2012. www.nprf.ie/Publications/2012/NPRFQ3 PerformancePortfolioOct2012.pdf.

21 K. Whelan, 'What is Ireland's bank debt and what can be done about it?', on Karl Whelan blog, 7 June 2012. http://karlwhelan.com/blog/?tag=bank-debt

22 'Names of top ten borrowers in first waves of Nama transfers revealed', *Irish Times*, 18 February 2010.

23 Comptroller and Auditor General, *Special Report on National Assets Management Agency Management of Loans*, Dublin: Government Publications, February 2012, p. 10.

24 Correspondence from NAMA to Public Accounts Committee, 20 September 2012. www.oireachtas.ie/parliament/media/committees/pac/correspondence/2012-meeting512009/%5bPAC-R-589%5dCorrespondence-3A.3.pdf

25 Dáil Éireann Debates, Vol. 760, No. 2. Written Answers: National Assets Management Agency, 22 March 2012.

26 Dáil Éireann Debates, Vol. 768, No. 1, Written Answers: National Assets Management Agency, 12 June 2012, p. 144.

27 'Harry Crosbie reveals the truth about NAMA', *Politico.ie*, 5 October 2011. http://politico.ie/component/content/article/7927.html

Chapter 2

1 Interview, RTE, *The Week in Politics,* 12 June 2011.

2 'The big gamble – the inside story of the bank guarantee', *Irish Times*, 25 September 2010.

3 *Opinion of the European Central Bank on the Draft Credit Institutions Bill* (CON/2008/44), 3 October 2008, p. 2.

4 Ibid., p. 3.

5 European Commission, *Guarantee Scheme for Banks in Ireland,* NN/48 13-10-2008, p. 12; my italics.

6 See G. Tett, *Fool's Gold: How Unrestrained Greed Corrupted a Dream, Shattered Global Markets and Unleashed a Catastrophe*, London: Abacus Books, 2009, for a useful account of this process.

7 Ibid., p. 204.

8 University of Iowa Center for International Finance and Development, 'Credit crunch: how US and European banks became involved in the financial crisis'. http://ebook.law.uiowa.edu/ebook/sites/default/files/Credit_Crunch.pdf

9 P. Honohan, 'Resolving Ireland's banking crisis', *The Economic and Social Review*, Vol. 40, No. 2, p. 218.

10 International Banking and Financial Developments, *Bank of International Settlements Quarterly Review,* June 2010, pp. 19–21.

11 R. Peet, *Unholy Trinity – The IMF, World Bank and WTO* (2nd ed.), London: Zed Books, 2009, p. 71.

12 N. Roubini and S. Mihm, *Crisis Economics – A Crash Course in the Future of Finance,* London: Penguin, p. 25.

13 R. Peet, *Unholy Trinity – The IMF, World Bank and WTO,* p. 84.

14 Institute of Latin American Studies, *The Debt Crisis in Latin America,* 1986, p. 69.

15 D. Harvey, *A Brief History of Neoliberalism,* Oxford: Oxford University Press, 2005, p. 29.

16 Ibid.

17 Ibid.

18 R. Peet, *Unholy Trinity – The IMF, World Bank and WTO,* p. 87.

19 Ibid.

20 J. Williamson, 'A short history of the Washington Consensus', *Peter G. Peterson Institute for International Economics,* 2004, pp. 3–4.

21 K. Watkins, 'Debt relief for Africa', *Review of African Political Economy,* 64, 1994, p. 126.

22 Share the World's Resources, *Financing the Global Sharing Economy,* London: STWR, 2012, p. 153.

23 'Transforming the Enhanced Structural Adjustment Facility (ESAF) and the Debt Initiative for the Heavily Indebted Poor Countries', *IMF Papers,* 2000, p. 1.

24 H. Kohler, 'Breaking the cycle of world poverty', *IMF Papers,* 2001, p. 1.

25 UNCTAD, *'The Least Developed Countries 2000 Report,* New York: United Nations, p. 110.

26 J. Stiglitz, *Globalisation and Its Discontents',* London: Penguin, 2002, p. 16.

27 B. T. Johnson and B. D. Schaefer, 'The International Monetary Fund: outdated, ineffective and unnecessary', Washington DC: Heritage Foundation, p. 54.

28 D. Budhoo, 'IMF/World Bank Wreak Havoc on the Third World', in K. Danaher, *50 Years Is Enough,* Boston, MA: South End Press, pp. 20–1.

29 R. Peet, *Unholy Trinity – The IMF, World Bank and WTO,* p. 105.

30 R. Peet, *Unholy Trinity – The IMF, World Bank and WTO,* p. 159.

31 Ibid.

32 R. Patel, 'They also make bombs out of paper', *ZNet,* 28 November 2001.

33 D. Harvey, *A Brief History of Neoliberalism,* Oxford: Oxford University Press, 2005, p. 162.

34 Ibid.

35 K. Danaher, *10 Reasons to Abolish the IMF & World Bank,* New York: Seven Stories Press, p. 62.

36 According to the *Financial Times,* 72 of the largest 100 European corporations are based in France, Germany or the UK (including the largest

seven). This gives them incredible power in the integration process. See: http://specials.ft.com/ft500/may2001/FT3MY20HKMC.html for more details.

37 G. Carcedi, *For Another Europe: A Class Analysis of European Economic Integration*, London: Verso, p. 1.

38 Quoted in Corporate European Observatory, *Corporate Europa*, Brussels: CEO, January 2011, p. 3.

39 Speech by Herman Van Rompuy, 11 November 2011. See: www.consilium.europa.eu/uedocs/cms_data/docs/pressdata/en/ec/126026.pdf for more details.

40 O. Onaran, 'Fiscal crisis or crisis of distribution', Discussion Paper 18, *Research on Money and Finance*, 2010, p. 8.

41 C. Lapavitsas, 'Working people have no interest in saving the Euro', *International Socialism*, Winter 2012, 130, p. 60.

42 C. Lapavitsas *et al.*, *Crisis in the Eurozone*, London: Verso, 2012, p. 31.

43 Ibid., p. 87.

44 'Draghi's $158 billion free lunch for European banks seen boosting profits', *Bloomberg*, 13 February 2012.

45 European Commission, *Ireland's Economic Crisis – How Did It Happen and What Is Being Done About It?* http://ec.europa.eu/ireland/economy/irelands_economic_crisis/index_en.htm

46 'Finance Department denies bailout report', *RTE News*, 15 November 2010.

47 'Letters show extent of pressure put on Lenihan for bailout', *Irish Times*, 1 September 2012.

48 Ibid.

49 'Portugal gives green light to €78bn EU/IMF bailout', *Irish Examiner*. www.irishexaminer.com/EUinireland/storyexaminer.aspx?id=153519

50 This rate has since been reduced under pressure from the working class in Greece, but the principle of the Troika benefiting from the Irish crisis remains unchanged.

51 'Who are the bondholders Ireland won't burn?' www.diarmaidcondon.com/who-are-the-bondholders-ireland-wont-burn/

52 'ECB affirms: investors won't lend to you if you burn bondholders', *The Journal*, 23 January 2012.

53 J. Asmussen, 'The Irish case from an ECB perspective', speech at the *Institute of European and International Affairs*, 12 April 2012.

Chapter 3

1 'Winning Merkel's praise', *Der Spiegel*, 15 November 2011.

2 'Noonan: we are not Greece . . . put that on a t-shirt', *Irish Independent*, 23 June 2011.

3 'IMF praises Ireland's attempts to rein in finances but warns of tough times ahead', *Irish Independent,* 5 October 2011.

4 EU Commission, *Economic Adjustment Programme for Ireland, Summer Review 2011,* Brussels: EU Commission Directorate General for Economic and Financial Affairs, 2011.

5 'Irish bailout cheapest in the world', *Irish Times,* 24 October 2008.

6 Standard & Poor's, 'Explaining Standard & Poor's adjustments to Ireland's public debt data', 24 August 2010.

7 'Stephen Donnelly: Europe must see a failed Ireland is bad for everyone', *Irish Independent,* 2 September 2012.

8 A. Barrett, I. Kearney, I. Goggin and T. Confrey, *Quarterly Economic Commentary,* Spring 2010, Dublin: ESRI, 2010, p. 7.

9 J. Fitzgerald and I. Kearney, 'Irish government debt and implied debt dynamics: 2011 to 2015', in J. Durkan, D. Duffy and C. O'Sullivan (eds), *Quarterly Economic Commentary,* Autumn 2011, Dublin ESRI, 2011, p. 27.

10 K. Whelan, *Ireland's Sovereign Debt Crisis,* Dublin: UCD Centre for Economic Research, 2011 Working Paper Series, p. 7.

11 CSO, *Quarterly National Account, Q3 2012,* Dublin: CSO, 2012, Table 1.

12 IBEC, *Supplementary Budget Proposals,* Dublin: IBEC, 2009, p. 4.

13 OECD, *Government at a Glance,* Paris: OECD, 2011, Chapter 6.

14 M. Taft, 'April 27th Morning: Recession Diaries', Notes from the Front, 27 April 2009. http://notesonthefront.typepad.com/politicaleconomy/2009/04/ronan-lyon-has-written-an-instructive-post-on-the-thorny-issue-of-teachers-pay-so-useful-in-fact-that-it-was-hig.html

15 J. Fitzgerald, 'How Ireland can stage an economic recovery', *Irish Times,* 24 January 2009.

16 CSO, *Industrial Earnings and Hours Worked,* Dublin: CSO, 2007, Table 5.

17 'Currency devaluation may look an easy option but it is a trick on workers', *Irish Independent,* 26 February 2009.

18 CSO, *Survey on Income and Living Conditions 2011 and Revised 2010 Results,* Dublin: CSO, 2013, Table 1, p. 8.

19 'Workers in Ireland and the Baltic states hit most by pay cuts', *Industrial Relations News,* No. 42, 17, November 2010.

20 CSO, *Quarterly National Accounts, Q3 2012,* Table 1.

21 R. Wright, *Strengthening the Capacity of the Department of Finance: Report of Independent Review Panel,* Dublin: Government Publications 2010, pp. 6 and 45.

22 ESRI, *Quarterly Economic Commentary,* Spring 2008, Dublin, ESRI, p. 1.

23 Irish Tax Institute, *Budget 2013,* Dublin: ITI, 2012, p. 3.

24 Revenue Commissioners, *Statistical Report 2011,* Dublin: Revenue Commissioners 2012, Table ISDI.

25 A. Barrett and C. Wall, *The Distributional Impact of Ireland's Indirect Tax System,* Dublin: Institute of Public Administration, 2006.

26 A. Decoster, J. Loughrey, C. O'Donoghue and D. Verwerft, 'How regressive are indirect taxes? A micro simulation analysis for five European countries', *Journal of Policy Analysis and Management*, Vol. 29, No. 2, 2010, pp. 326–350, p. 335.

27 A. Barrett, and C. Wall, *The Distributional Impact of Ireland's Indirect Tax System*, p. 8.

28 Public Health Policy Centre, *All Ireland Policy Paper on Fuel Poverty and Health*, Dublin: Institute of Public Health, 2007.

29 Social Justice Ireland, *Budget 2013 Analysis and Critique,* Dublin: Social Justice Ireland, 2012, p. 9.

30 K. Allen, *The Celtic Tiger: The Myth of Social Partnership*, Manchester: Manchester University Press, 2000.

31 'Number on hospital waiting lists up 20,000', *Irish Times,* 14 November 2012.

32 CSO, *Survey on Income and Living Conditions (2010)*, Dublin: CSO, 2012, Table 1A.

33 Ibid.

34 Oireachtas Library and Research Service, *Debt Part 2: Personal Debt and Consequences*, Dublin: Houses of Oireachtas, 2010.

35 CSO, *Institutional Sector Non-Financial and Financial Accounts 2011*, Dublin: CSO, 2012, Table 5.

36 Bank of Ireland, *Wealth of the Nation*, Dublin: Bank of Ireland 2007.

37 CSO, *Institutional Sector Accounts,* Dublin: CSO, 2011, p. 7.

38 CSO, *Institutional Sector Accounts Non-Financial and Financial 2011*, Dublin: CSO, 2012, p. 8.

39 Ibid., p. 9.

Chapter 4

1 www.youtube.com/watch?v=1yeA_kHHLow

2 N. Klein, *The Shock Doctrine*, London: Allen Lane, 2007.

3 CSO, *The Roof Over Our Heads*, Dublin: CSO, 2012, p. 12.

4 Society of Chartered Surveyors Ireland, *Creating a Fair, Sustainable and Transparent Property Taxation System*, Dublin: SCSI, 2012, p. 7.

5 J. Arnold, *Do Tax Structures Affect the Aggregate Economic Growth? Empirical Evidence from a Panel of OECD Countries',* Working Paper 643, Paris: OECD 2008.

6 TASC Submission to the Inter-Departmental Group on Property Tax, March 2012. www.tascnet.ie/upload/file/Property%20Tax%20Upload.pdf

7 D. Thornhill, *Design of a Local Property Tax: Report of the Inter-Departmental Group*, Dublin: Government Publications, 2012, p. 77.

8 'Property tax isn't so bad if you're sitting in a mansion on 150 acres', *Irish Independent,* 10 March 2013.

9 *Commission on Taxation Report*, Dublin: Government Publications, 2008, p. 167.

10 *Commission on Taxation*, p. 161 and Thornhill, *Design of a Local Property Tax*, p. 29.

11 Finance (Local Property Tax) Bill 2012, Article 12, p. 16.

12 Ibid., Article 42, p. 26.

13 Fine Gael, *Let's Get Ireland Working: Election Manifesto*, Dublin: Fine Gael, 2011, p. 66.

14 Labour Party, *One Ireland: Jobs, Reform and Fairness,* Dublin: Labour Party, 2011, p. 16.

15 Thornhill, *Design of a Local Property Tax*, p. 49.

16 Ibid., p. 23.

17 Ibid., p. 23.

18 Department of Environment, Community and Local Government, *Reform of the Water Sector in Ireland*, Dublin: 2012, p. 6.

19 PricewaterhouseCoopers, *Irish Water: Phase 1 Report*, Dublin: PWC, 2012, p. 12.

20 Department of Environment, Community and Local Government, *Reform of the Water Sector in Ireland: Position Paper*, Dublin: DECLG, 2012, p. 14

21 EU/IMF *Programme of Support for Ireland*, 2010, p. 9.

22 PWC, *Irish Water: Phase 1 Report*, p. 22.

23 C. Shaddon, 'Do water meters reduce domestic consumption? A summary of available literature', Heterodox Economics for Environment and Development Network, 2010, p. 9. www.heednet.org/metering-defraHEEDnet.pdf

24 Ibid., pp. 3–4.

25 A. Walker, *Independent Review of Charging for Household Water and Sewerage*, London: DEFRA, 2009, p. 74.

26 Department of Environment Briefing Document on Decision to Establish Irish Water as a Subsidiary of Bord Gais Eireann: Questions and Answers, p. 10. www.environ.ie/en/Publications/. . ./Water/FileDownLoad,29945,en.d

27 Shaddon, 'Do water meters reduce. . . ?', p. 5.

28 PWC, *Irish Water*, p. 15.

29 G. A. Hodge and C. Greve, 'Public Private Partnerships – an international performance review', *Public Administration Review*, May/June 2007, pp. 545–58.

30 Oxfam, *Land and Power Briefing Paper 151*, London: Oxfam, 2011, p. 2.

31 Quoted in *Report of Review Group on State Assets and Liabilities (McCarthy Report)*, Dublin: Department of Finance, 2011, p. 7. IMF, *Ireland: Request for an Extended Arrangement—Staff Report*, December 2010, p. 56.

32 'TDs cut and Run as 3,000 jobs lost a week', *Irish Independent*, 5 July 2009.

33 'IMF pushes for fire sale of assets', *Irish Examiner,* 8 September 2011.

34 *Report of Review Group on State Assets and Liabilities (McCarthy Report)*, Dublin: Department of Finance, 2011, p. 75.

35 *Report of Review Group on State Assets and Liabilities*, p. 76.

36 Department of Agriculture, Fisheries and Food, 'Submission on Coillte to the Review Group on State Assets and Liabilities, September 2010, p. 4.

37 Independent Panel on Forestry, *Final Report*, London: DEFRA, 2012, p. 19.

38 Ibid., p. 25.

39 Ibid., p. 28.

40 National Youth Council, *Youth Unemployment: The Forgotten Generation*, Dublin: NYC, 2010, p. 9.

41 Article 1. 15 Croke Park Agreement, p. 6. http://per.gov.ie/wp-content/uploads/Public-Service-Agreement-2010-2014-Final-for-print-June-2010.pdf

42 *Pathways to Work: Government Policy on Labour Activation*, Dublin: Government of Ireland, 2012, p. 8.

43 Ibid., p. 12.

44 Department of Social Protection, *High Level Issues Paper Emanating from a Review of Department of Social Protection Employment Support Schemes*, Dublin: DSE, 2012, p. 18.

45 Ibid., p. 24.

46 Ibid., p. 25.

47 Ibid., p. 35.

48 'Five myths about internships', *Washington Post*, 13 May 2011.

49 'A small slice of workplace life', in *Notes from the Front*, 18 November 2012. http://notesonthefront.typepad.com/politicaleconomy/2012/11/a-small-slice-of-workplace-life.html

50 'Internships could lead to exploitation: IMPACT', *RTE News*, 12 May 2011.

51 'State's JobBridge scheme suffers 75% drop-out rate', *Sunday Times*, 6 May 2012.

Chapter 5

1 'The return of the American wake', *Donegal Democrat*, 18 January 2011.

2 CSO, *Quarterly National Household Survey: Educational Attainment, Thematic Report 2011*, Dublin: CSO, 2011, Table 12b.

3 M. Taft, 'The unemployment crisis: a modest 0.7% response', in *Notes from the Front*. http://notesonthefront.typepad.com/politicaleconomy/2012/11/even-the-government-admits-their-policies-are-having-little-effect-on-job-creation-they-expect-unemployment-to-remain-at-1-1.html

4 Department of Enterprise, Trade and Employment, *Action Plan for Jobs 2012*, Dublin: DETE, 2102, p. 7.

5 CSO, *Quarterly National Household Survey Q3 2012* and CSO, *Revisions to Labour Market Estimates*, November 2012.

6 Department of Social Protection, *Fraud Initiative 2011–2013*, Dublin, Department of Social Protection, 2011, p. 1., Minister's Foreword.

7 Oireachtas Library and Research Services Spotlight, *Tracking Social Welfare Fraud No. 5*, Dublin: Government Publications, 2011, p. 8.

8 Comptroller and Auditor General, *Annual Report 2011*, Dublin: Government Publications, 2011, Chapter 22, p. 291.

9 T. Callan, J. Walsh and K. Coleman, *Modelling Tax and Welfare Policy in Ireland*, Dublin: ESRI, 2005.

10 Estimates for Public Services and Summary Public Capital Programme, 2011, p. 38. http://budget.gov.ie/budgets/2011/Documents/Estimates%20Budget%202011.pdf

11 Department of Social Protection, *Family Income Supplement Uptake Research*, Dublin: Department of Social Protection, 2008, p. 10.

12 OECD Family Database, Net replacement rates for six family types. www.oecd.org/els/socialpoliciesanddata/NRR_Initial_EN.xlsx

13 The number of member countries in the European Union prior to the accession of ten candidate countries on 1 May 2004.

14 OECD Family Database, net replacement rates for six family types.

15 'Burton vows to end "dole lifestyle choice"', *Irish Independent*, 17 July 2011.

16 Nevin Economic Research Institute, *Quarterly Economic Facts Spring 2012*, Dublin: NERI, 2012, p. 30.

17 Ibid., p. 28.

18 CSO, *Quarterly National Household Survey Q3 2012*, Dublin: CSO, 2012, p. 1.

19 L. Jacobson, R. LaLonde and D. Sullivan, 'Earnings losses of displaced workers', *American Economic Review*, Vol. 83, No. 4, 1993, pp. 685–709, and T. von Wachter, J. Song and J. Manchester, 'Long-term earnings losses due to mass-layoffs during the 1982 recession: an analysis using longitudinal administrative data from 1974 to 2004', Mimeo, Columbia University, New York, 2009.

20 D. Sullivan and T. von Wachter, 'Job displacement and mortality: an analysis using administrative data', *Quarterly Journal of Economics*, August 2009.

21 H. Kuper and M. Marmot, 'Job strain, job demands, decision latitude, and risk of coronary heart disease within the Whitehall II study', *Journal of Epidemiology and Community Health*, Vol. 57, No. 2, 2003, pp. 147–53.

22 A. Stevens and J. Schaller, 'Short-run effects of parental job loss on children's academic achievement', *NBER Working Paper* No. 15480, Cambridge, Massachusetts, 2009.

23 M. Palme and S. Sandgren, 'Parental income, lifetime income, and mortality', *Journal of the European Economic Association*, Vol. 6, No. 4, 2008, pp. 890–911.

24 M. Jahoda, P. Lazaersfeld, and H. Zeisel, *Marienthal: The Sociography of an Unemployed Community*, New Brunswick: Transaction Books, 2009.

25 M. Jahoda and H. Rush, 'Work, employment and unemployment: an overview of ideas and research results in the social science literature'.

Occasional Paper Series, No. 12, Science Policy Research Unit, University of Sussex, 1980. Quoted in Winefield, A., Tiggemann, M. and H. Winefield, 'Spare time use and psychological well-being in employed and unemployed young people', *Journal of Occupational & Organizational Psychology*, Vol. 65, No. 4, 1992, pp. 307–13.

26 J. Brand and S. Burgard, 'Job displacement and social participation over the lifecourse: findings for a cohort of joiners', *Social Forces*, Vol. 87, No. 1, 2008, pp. 211–42.

27 D. Dooley, R. Catalano and R. Hough, 'Unemployment and alcohol disorder in 1910 and 1990: drift versus social causation', *Journal of Occupational and Organizational Psychology*, Vol. 65, No. 4, 1992, pp. 277–90.

28 K. K. Charles and M. Stephens Jr., 'Job displacement, disability, and divorce', *Journal of Labor Economics*, Vol. 22, No. 2, 2004, pp. 489–522.

29 M. Davis, 'Spring confronts winter', *New Left Review* 72, November–December 2011, pp. 12–13.

30 IMF, *Ireland: Sixth Review under Extended Agreement*, IMF Country Report 12/147, June 2012, p. 32.

Chapter 6

1 Central Bank, *Residential Mortgage Arrears and Repossession Statistics Q4, 2012*, Dublin: Central Bank, 2013.

2 Davy Stockbrokers, *Research Report: Irish Mortgage Arrears Analysis*, Dublin: Davy Stockbrokers, 17 August 2012, p. 9.

3 Central Bank, *Residential Mortgage Arrears and Repossession Statistics Q4, 2012*.

4 Davy Stockbrokers, *Research Report: Irish Mortgage Arrears Analysis*, 17 August 2012.

5 Address by Director of Credit Institutions and Insurance Supervision Fiona Muldoon to the Irish Banking Federation National Conference 2012.

6 See Transcript of John Moran at Dail Public Accounts Finance Committee on Sean Whelan, RTE Economics Correspondent blog. www.rte.ie/blogs/business/2013/03/13/repo-man/

7 IMF, *Ireland: Eighth Review under the Extended Arrangement*, Washington: IMF, 2012, p. 19.

8 Central Bank, *Review of Code of Conduct on Mortgage Arrears*, Dublin: Central Bank, 2013.

9 T. Guo, 'Tenants at foreclosure: mitigating harm to innocent victims of the foreclosure crisis', *DePaul Journal for Social Justice*, No. 4, 2011.

10 Davy Stockbrokers, *Irish Mortgage Arrears*, p. 5.

11 R. Kitchin, J. Gleeson, K. Keaveney and C. O'Callaghan, *A Haunted Landscape: Housing and Ghost Estates in Post Celtic Tiger Ireland*, Maynooth: NIRSA, 2010, p. 17.

12 Ibid., p. 10.
13 An Taisce, *State of the Nation: A Review of Ireland's Planning System 2000–2011*, Dublin: An Taisce, 2012, p.19.
14 Pyrite Action Group, Submission to the Joint Oireachtas Committee on Environment, Transport, Culture and Gaeltacht, 11 October 2011.
15 An Taisce, *State of the Nation*, p. 31.
16 Department of the Environment, *Resolving Ireland's Unfinished Housing Developments*, Dublin: DOE, 2011, p. 4.

Chapter 7

1   CSO, *Estimates of the Capital Stock of Fixed Assets*, Dublin: CSO, 2011, Table 1.
2   NCB, *2020 Vision: Ireland's Demographic Dividend*, Dublin: NCB, 2006, p. 140.
3   S. Kelly, *Breakfast with Anglo*, Dublin: Penguin, Ireland, 2010, p. 36.
4   T. Lyons and B. Carey, *The Fitzpatrick Tapes*, Dublin: Penguin, Ireland, 2011, p. 32.
5   Ibid., p. 45.
6   K. Regling and M. Watson, *A Preliminary Report on the Sources of Ireland's Banking Crisis*, Dublin: Government Publications, 2011, p. 31.
7   Lyons and Carey, *The Fitzpatrick Tapes*, p. 47.
8   National Economic and Social Council, *A Review of Industrial Policy: A Report Prepared by the Telesis Consultancy Group*, Dublin: NESC, 1983.
9   Forfas, *Ireland's Productivity Performance 1980–2011*, Dublin: Forfas, 2012, p. 25, Table 1.
10 'Is Big Pharma about to take a fall?', *Irish Times*, 2 March 2012.
11 'Ireland faces a $26 billion export headache as drugs stop working', *Bloomberg*, 22 November 2011.
12 D. Bell, *The Coming of the Post Industrial Society: A Venture in Social Forecasting*, New York: Basic Books, 1976.
13 P. Bacon, *Overcapacity in the Irish Hotel Industry and the Required Elements of a Recovery Programme*, Dublin: Irish Hotel Federation, 2009.
14 S. O'Riain, 'An offshore Silicon Valley? The emerging Irish software industry', *Competition and Change*, No. 2, 199, pp. 175–212.
15 S. O'Riain, *From Developmental Network State to Market Managerialism in Ireland*, Kildare: NUIM Sociology, 2009.
16 'Multinationals benefit as their financial advisers pile pressure on governments', *Irish Times*, 22 April 2012.
17 Ibid.
18 Ibid.
19 G. Lewis, 'Quintin McGarel Hogg, Lord Hailsham of St Marylebone', in *Biographical Memoirs of Fellows of the Royal Society*, London: Royal Society 2002, p. 226.

20 S. Klinger, C. Collins and H. Sklar, *Unfair Advantage: The Business Case against Overseas Tax Havens*, New York: American Sustainable Business Council, 2010, p. 3.

21 Ibid.

22 PIRG, *Tax Shell Game: What Do Tax Dodgers Cost You?*, Washington: PIRG, 2010, p. 1.

23 US Government Accountability Office, *US Multinational Corporations: Effective Tax Rates Are Correlated with Where Income Is Reported*, Washington: GAO, 2008, p. 4.

24 N. Shaxson, *Treasure Islands: Tax Havens and the Men Who Stole the World*, London: Bodley Head, 2011.

25 R. Palen, R. Murphy and C. Chavagneux, *Tax Havens: How Globalisation Really Works*, New York: Cornell University, 2010, p. 51.

26 J. Henry, *The Price of Offshore Revisited*, London: Tax Justice Network, 2012.

27 OECD, *Harmful Tax Competition: An Emerging Global Issue*, Paris: OECD, 1998.

28 N. Johannesen and G. Zucman, *The End of Bank Secrecy? An Evaluation of the G20 Tax Haven Crackdown*, Paris: Paris School of Economics Working Papers No. 2012–4, 2012, p. 4.

29 Grant Thornton, *Hedge Fund Adviser,* February, 2011.

30 Transnational Institute, *Countering Illicit and Unregulated Money Flows: Money Laundering, Tax Evasion and Financial Regulation*, Amsterdam: Transnational Institute, 2009, p. 18.

31 'Romney reports income funds from Goldman, Golden Gate', *Bloomberg.com,* 25 January 2012; 'Ireland listed as a tax haven by Obama re-election campaign team', *RTE.ie*, 6 July 2012.

32 'Obama forced to retract allegation that Ireland is a tax haven', *Irish Independent*, 27 July 2012.

33 Tax Strategy Group, Briefing Document on International Tax Policy: Tax Havens and Related Tax Policy Issues TSG09/16a, pp. 4–5.

34 See OECD Tax Database. www.oecd.org/document/60/0,3746,en_2649_37427_1942460_1_1_1_37427,00.html#C_CorporateCaptia

35 Minutes of the Main TALC Meeting, 19 September 2012. www.revenue.ie/en/practitioner/talc/talc-minutes-190912.pdf

36 Ibid.

37 E. Kleinbard, 'Stateless income', Special Issue of *Florida Tax Review*, Vol. 11, No. 9, 2011, p. 720.

38 'At big US companies, 60% of cash sits offshore', *Wall Street Journal*, 17 May 2012.

39 'Tax wars: the accidental billion dollar tax break', *Financial Times*, 27 September 2011.

40 Ibid.

41 Deloitte, *Transfer Pricing Legislation in Ireland – A New Reality*, Dublin: Deloitte, 2010, p. 48.

42 Quoted in D. Spencer, 'Transfer pricing: will the OECD adjust to reality?', *Tax Justice Network*, 24 May 2012.

43 *Tax Justice Network*, Statement on Transfer Pricing, 21 March 2012.

44 'Apple just one of many companies which avail of offshore tax arrangements', *Irish Times*, 31 May 2013.

45 M. Everett, 'The statistical implications of multinational companies' corporate structures', *Central Bank Quarterly Bulletin*, April 2012, pp. 59–61.

46 'Report: Repatriation tax holiday: a failed policy', *Wall Street Journal*, 10 October 2011.

47 J. Gravelle, *Tax Havens: International Tax Avoidance and Evasion*, Washington: Congressional Research Service, 2010, p. 20.

48 *Implementing the Information Society in Ireland: An Action Plan*, Dublin: Department of the Taoiseach, 1999, p. 2.

49 For more details, see the 'Delta' example used in a Joint Committee on Taxation Report on Present Law and Background Related to Possible Income Shifting and Transfer Pricing, Washington, 2010, pp. 77–83.

50 PWC, *Generating Cash from Irish R&D Activities*, Dublin: PWC, 2011, p. 1.

51 'US companies dodge $60 billion in taxes with global odyssey', *Bloomberg*, 13 May 2010.

52 'IRS: Boston Scientific owes $581 million in back taxes', *Minneapolis St Paul Business Journal*, 7 December 2011.

53 'Google 2.4% rate shows how $60 billion lost to tax loopholes', *Bloomberg*, 21 October 2010.

54 'Irish subsidiary let Microsoft slash taxes in US and Europe', *Wall Street Journal*, 7 November 2005.

55 Memorandum on Offshore Profit Shifting and US Tax Code for US Senate Permanent Subcommittee on Investigation, 20 September 2012.

56 Memorandum on Offshore Profit Shifting and US Tax Code for US Senate Permanent Subcommittee on Investigation, 21 May 2013.

57 'US medical giant Boston Scientific paid effective tax rate of 4% in 2011', *Irish Times*, 31 May 2013.

58 'Pepsi firm with $1bn assets pays taxes in Curaco [*sic*]', *Irish Independent*, 2 June 2013.

59 'GE's strategies let it avoid taxes altogether', *New York Times*, 24 March 2011.

60 'Pre-tax profits of €606 million for aviation leasing firm', *Irish Times*, 20 June 2012.

61 D. MacKenzie, 'An address in Mayfair', *London Review of Books*, Vol. 30, No. 23, December 2008, pp. 9–12.

62 Accenture. *The IFSC: The International Financial Services Sector in Ireland*, Dublin: Accenture, 2010, p.13.

63 Matheson, *Ireland: The SPV Jurisdiction of Choice for Structured Finance,* Transactions Dublin: Matheson, 2013, p. 2.

64 Arthur Cox, *Establishing Special Purpose Vehicles in Ireland for Structured Finance Transactions,* May 2011.

65 J. Stewart, 'Low tax financial centres and the financial crisis: the case of the Irish Financial Services Centre', IIIS Discussion Paper 420. www.tcd.ie/iiis/documents/discussion/pdfs/iiisdp420.pdf

66 Dillon Eustace, *Investment Funds Listing on the Irish Stock Exchange,* Dublin: Dillon Eustace, no date, pp. 3, 4.

67 'Central Bank takes back ISE probe tasks', *RTE.ie,* 31 January 2012.

68 Written Answers, Department of the Taoiseach, 13 March 2012.

69 Dáil Éireann, Written Answers – Financial Regulation, 15 December 2011, 40673/11.

Chapter 8

1   'We may top the austerity class but the pain is very real', *Irish Times,* 8 December 2012.

2   M. Marsh, R. Sinnot, J. Garry and F. Kennedy, *The Irish Voter: The Nature of Electoral Competition in the Republic of Ireland,* Manchester: Manchester University Press, 2008, p. 5.

3   'Enda Kenny welcomes "democratic revolution"', *RTE.ie,* 28 February 2011. www.rte.ie/news/2011/0226/298076-politics/

4   R. Bruton, 'Time for new politics', *Business and Finance,* May 2010.

5   'David McWilliams: The "Rock Star" Economist'. www.mediabite.org/article_The—Rock-Star—Economist_384381524.html

6   Fine Gael, *New Politics,* Dublin: Fine Gael, 2010.

7   Ibid., p. 25.

8   'Triumphant Labour emerges from wilderness of opposition', *Irish Times,* 16 April 2012. 'Labour haunted by old slogans', *Irish Independent,* 12 May 2012.

9   Dáil Debates, Vol. 725, No. 2, 15 December 2010.

10 'Dead hand of cronyism evident in jobs for party apparatchiks', *Irish Times,* 11 June 2012.

11 'Shatter and cronyism row', Tales from Talbot Tower – Blog of journalist Ken Foxe, 20 June 2011. www.kenfoxe.com/

12 'Westport's Durcan appointed District Court Judge', *Mayo News,* 8 November 2011.

13 'Lawyer with links to Gilmore gets top judge job', *Irish Independent,* 13 October 2011.

14 'Kenny faces Dail quiz on judicial appointments', *Irish Independent,* 26 September 2012.

15 *Report of the Tribunal of Inquiry into Payments to Politicians and Related Matters, Part 2,* Dublin: Government Publications, 2012, p. 1157.

16 Ibid.

17 G. Di Lampedusa, *The Leopard*, London: Fontana, 1963, p. 29.

18 'Pension entitlements multiply Ministers' pay', *Irish Times*, 30 October 2012.

19 'Anne Harris: O'Brien – the real issue is press freedom', *Irish Independent*, 17 June 2012.

20 'Best value for money in a paper is truth', *Irish Independent*, 15 April 2012.

21 C. Crouch, *Post Democracy*, Oxford: Polity, 2004, and S. Wollin, *Democracy Incorporated: Managed Democracy and the Specter of Inverted Totalitarianism*, Princeton: Princeton University Press, 2010.

22 P. Mair, 'Ruling the void: the hollowing out of Western democracy', *New Left Review 46*, November–December 2006, pp. 25–51.

23 *Report of the Tribunal of Inquiry into the Payment of Politicians and Related Matters, Part 2*, Volume 2, Dublin: Moriarty Tribunal, 2012, p. 1951.

24 J. Whyte, 'Ireland: politics without social bases', in R. Rose, *Electoral Behaviour: A Comparative Handbook*, New York: The Free Press, p. 619.

25 J. Coakley, 'The election and the party system', in M. Gallagher, M. Marsh and P. Mitchell, *How Ireland Voted 2002*, Basingstoke: Palgrave Macmillan, 2003, pp. 231–32.

26 M. Gallagher and M. Marsh, *How Ireland Voted 2007: The Full Story of Ireland's General Election*, Basingstoke: Palgrave Macmillan, 2008, p. 222.

27 D. Walsh, *The Party: Inside Fianna Fail*, Dublin: Gill and Macmillan, 1986, p. 32; J. P. Carroll. 'Eamon de Valera, charisma and political development', in J. P. Carroll and J. A. Murphy (eds), *De Valera and His Times*, Cork: Cork University Press, 1983, p. 33.

28 Dáil Debates, Vol. 25, Col. 478, 12 July 1928.

29 Quoted in T. Ryle Dwyer, *De Valera*, Dublin: Poolbeg, 1991, p. 134.

30 J. A. Murphy, *Ireland in the Twentieth Century*, Cork: Mercier, 1981, p. 86.

31 National Economic and Social Council, *A Review of Industrial Policy (Telesis Report)*, Dublin: NESC, 1982, pp. 187–8.

32 Dáil Debates, Vol. 31, Col. 397, 26 October 1927.

33 M. Gallagher, *Political Parties in the Republic of Ireland*, Dublin: Gill and Macmillan, 1985, p. 27.

34 M. Marsh, 'Explanations for party choice', in M. Gallagher and M. Marsh, *How Ireland Voted 2007*, p. 117.

35 A wealthy part of Dublin, also known as Dublin 4 after its postal address.

36 Gallagher, *Political Parties*, p. 44 and p. 66.

37 Ibid., p. 47.

38 Ibid., p. 61.

39 M. Manning, *The Blueshirts*, Dublin: Gill and Macmillan, 1987.

40 ITUC, *Annual Report and Conference Proceedings*, Dublin: ITUC, 1934, p. 39.

41 K. Rafter, *Fine Gael: Party at the Crossroads*, Dublin: New Books, 2009, p. 164.

42 M. Gallagher and M. Marsh, *How Ireland Voted 2011: The Full Story of Ireland's Earthquake Election*, Basingstoke: Palgrave, 2011, p. 177.

43 Ibid., p. 179.

44 Ibid., p. 182.

45 'Fee paying schools have the edge on the battle for seats at the Cabinet', *Irish Independent*, 27 December 2012.

46 Dáil Debates, Vol. 34, Col. 318, 2 April 1930.

Chapter 9

1 'The burning question: Why don't we protest?', *Irish Independent*, 17 November 2012.

2 T. Boland, 'Why don't the Irish protest?', *South Eastern Sociology*, 7 November 2011.

3 'Pensioners jeer minister at 15,000-strong protest rally', *Irish Independent*, 23 October 2008.

4 CSO, *National Income and Expenditure Annual Results*, Dublin: CSO, 2004.

5 D. McWilliams, 'Robopaddy and the New Africa', *Sunday Business Post,* 27 June 2004.

6 L. Collins, 'Now the Irish are buying London – not building it', *Irish Independent,* 2 October 2005.

7 T. Fahey, H. Russell and C. Whelan, *Best of Times? The Social Impact of the Celtic Tiger,* Dublin: Institute of Public Administration, 2007, p. 138.

8 R. Foster, *Luck and the Irish*, Oxford: Oxford University Press, 2008, p. 32.

9 M. Riordan, *The Voice of a Thinking Intelligent Movement: James Larkin Junior and the Ideological Modernisation of Irish Trade Unionism*, Dublin: Irish Labour History Society, 1995.

10 N. Hardiman, 'Politics and social partnership: flexible network governance', *Economic and Social Review*, Vol. 37, No. 3, 2006, pp. 343–74.

11 N. Hardiman, 'Social partnership, wage bargaining and growth', pp. 286–309, in Brian Nolan, Philip O'Connell and Christopher T. Whelan (eds), *Bust to Boom: The Irish Experience of Growth and Inequality,* Dublin: Institute of Public Administration, 2008.

12 W. K. Roche, 2007, 'Social partnership in Ireland and new social pacts', *Industrial Relations,* Vol. 46, No. 3, pp. 395–425.

13 R. O'Donnell and C. O'Riordan, 'Social partnership in Ireland's economic transformation', pp. 237–56, in G. Fajertag and P. Poehet (eds), *Social Pacts in Europe: New Dynamics,* Brussels: European Trade Union Institute, 2000.

14 Roche, 'Social partnership in Ireland's economic transformation', p. 411.

15 'Congress starts internal analysis of partnership role of unions', *Industrial Relations News*, 20 January 2010.

16 B. Webb and S. Webb 1907, *A History of Trade Unionism,* London: Longman, 1907, p. 453.

17 A. Gramsci, 'Soviets in Italy', *New Left Review*, No. 51, 1968, pp. 25–58.

18 Central Statistics Office, *Quarterly National Household Survey: Union Membership Q2 2007*, Dublin: CSO, 2008, p. 5.

19 T. Dobbins, 'Irish industrial relations system no longer voluntarist', *Industrial Relations News*, 10, 3 March 2005.

20 P. Gunnigle, D. Collins and M. Morley, 'Hosting the multinational: exploring the dynamics of industrial relations in US multinational subsidiaries', in G. Boucher and G. Collins (eds), *Working in Ireland*, Dublin: Liffey Press, 2005, pp. 125–44.

21 W. K. Roche, 'Social partnership in Ireland and new social pacts', 2007, p. 403.

22 P. Sweeney, *Ireland's Economic Success: Reasons and Lessons*. Dublin: New Island, 2008, p. 125.

23 'FAS funds and SIPTU/ICTU', *The Story*, 6 September 2010. http://thestory.ie/2010/09/06/fas-funds-and-siptuictu/

24 'Inquiry into €1m lodged to union's account', *Irish Times*, 16 September 2011.

25 'Correspondence reveals how partnership money was put on "firm footing"', *Industrial Relations News*, No. 40, 3 November 2010.

26 'Political stability helps drive Irish recovery', *Financial Times*, 27 January 2012.

Chapter 10

1 J. Tonge, 'Sinn Fein and the "New Republicanism" in Belfast', *Space and Polity*, Vol. 10, No. 2, August 2007, pp. 135–47.

2 J. Evans and J. Tonge, 'From abstentionism to enthusiasm: Sinn Fein, nationalist electors and support for devolved power-sharing in Northern Ireland', *Irish Political Studies*, Vol. 28, No. 1, 2013, pp. 39–57.

3 Ibid.

4 B. Feeney, *Sinn Fein: A Hundred Turbulent Years*, Dublin: O'Brien, 2002, p. 436.

5 Sinn Fein, *Making the Right Choices: Sinn Fein Alternative Budget 2013*, Dublin: Sinn Fein, 2012, p. 3.

6 Ibid., pp. 4 and 5.

7 Sinn Fein, *Jobs Plan: Investing in Ireland's Future*, Dublin: Sinn Fein, 2012.

8 M. Marsh and K. Cunningham, 'A positive choice, or anyone but Fianna Fáil?', in M. Gallagher and M. Marsh (eds), *How Ireland Voted 2011: The Full Story of Ireland's Earthquake Election*, Basingstoke: Palgrave, 2011.

9 Red C General Election Opinion Poll, 24 February 2013.

10 Quoted in E. Moloney, *A Secret History of the IRA*, London: Allen Lane, 2002, p. 186.

11 R. Munck, 'Marxism and Northern Ireland', *Review of Radical Political Economics*, Vol. 13, No. 3, 1981.

12 J. Doyle, 'Republican policies in practical politics: placing contemporary Sinn Fein in a European context', Working papers in British-Irish Studies, UCD No. 45, 2005, p. 3.

13 Sinn Fein, *Getting Ireland Back to Work*, Dublin: Sinn Fein, 2009, p. 10.

14 Ibid.

15 Ibid., pp. 10, 12 and 14.

16 'Sinn Fein war chest swells as global ties pay dividends', *Irish Independent*, 4 March 2012.

17 'The radicalization of Peter King', *Mother Jones*, 20 December 2010.

18 M. Frampton, *The Long March: The Political Strategy of Sinn Fein 1981–2007*, London: Palgrave Macmillan, 2009, p. 149.

19 G. Horgan and J. S. O'Connor, 'Abortion and Citizenship Rights in a Devolved Region of the UK', *Social Policy and Society*, Vol. 12, No. 4, 2013.

20 G. Horgan and A. M. Gray, 'Devolution in Northern Ireland: a lost opportunity', *Critical Social Policy*, Vol. 32, No. 3, 2012, pp. 467–78.

21 T. Nairn, 'The modern Janus', *New Left Review*, Vol. 1, No. 94, November–December 1975, p. 12.

22 'General election not a beauty contest: Adams', *Irish Independent*, 5 January 2011.

23 E. O' Broin, *Sinn Fein and the Politics of Left Republicanism*, London: Pluto Press, 2009, p. 307.

24 K. Bean, *The New Politics of Sinn Fein*, Liverpool: Liverpool University Press, 2007, p. 190.

25 O' Broin, *Sinn Fein and the Politics of Left Republicanism*, p. 307.

26 Horgan and Gray, 'Devolution in Northern Ireland', p. 475.

27 S. McVeigh, 'Sinn Fein in government', *Irish Marxist Review*, Vol. 1, No. 1, 2012, pp. 34–40.

28 R. Murphy, *Pot of Gold or Fool's Gold*, Dublin: ICTU, 2010.

29 'Rage at Stormont over workfare (or not)', *Derry Journal*, 29 March 2012.

30 K. Allen, *Fianna Fail and Irish Labour*, London: Pluto Press, 1997.

Chapter 11

1 Oxfam Briefing Paper, *The Cost of Inequality: How Wealth and Income Extremes Hurt Us All*, 18 January 2013.

2 'Revealed: the capitalist network that controls the world', *New Scientist*, 24 October 2011.

3 Department of Communications, Energy and Natural Resources, *Strategy for Renewable Energy 2010–2012*, Dublin: DCENR, 2012, p. 7.

4 Shell to Sea, 'Liquid Assets Report', Dublin: Shell to Sea, 2012, p. 7.

5 D. Johnston, 'Changing fiscal landscape', *Journal of World Energy Law and Business*, Vol. 1, No. 1, 2008, pp. 31–54.

6 Indecon International Economic Consultants, *Expert Advice on Review of Irish Petroleum E&P Licensing Terms*, London: Indecon, 2007, p. 76.
7 Socialist Party statement on leaving ULA. www.socialistparty.net/component/content/article/1-latest-news/1123-the-ula-the-fight-against-austerity-a-building-a-new-party-of-the-working-class

Index